Gravity Goldberg is shining a light on the truth of what it means to be a teacher that makes a difference. Every child deserves one, and every teacher is capable of becoming one.

—Seth Godin
Author, *Linchpin*

Gravity Goldberg's Teach Like Yourself *offers a masterful instructional lens through which we get to view—and take on—a transformative process leading to professional ownership. Gravity dedicates her book to "brave" teachers everywhere and then shows us how to nurture our inner brave. Through her wisdom, we learn how to turn teaching inward, to our strengths and to discovering and nurturing our innermost beliefs about learning. Through this reflection rises new knowledge and renewed courage. Owning this book is like having Gravity Goldberg as our personal professional life coach, for she gently nudges us to authenticity while ever reminding us to keep self-care in our sights. Three simple but powerful words suddenly loom large and will inspire us all to bring her words to life: "You are enough."*

—Mary Howard, Education Consultant at Reading Partners
Author, *Good to Great Teaching*

Finally, a personal transformation guide for teachers! This crystal-clear, joyful antidote to scripted lessons and obsession with test scores will energize and inspire you to face your classroom tomorrow with a brave new heart. Gravity's honest, practical, research-based, and meaning-rich advice will help you be not only an authentic, happy teacher but also an authentic, happy person.

—Katherine Bomer
Author, *Hidden Gems: Naming and Teaching from the Brilliance in Every Student's Writing*

Gravity Goldberg's book provides an essential teacher guide to self-reflection. It offers challenging questions we must consider in order to be effective and fulfilled teachers over the long term.

—Larry Ferlazzo, High School Teacher
EdWeek Columnist and Author

I love this book! Gravity Goldberg addresses many important issues of our profession during this digital age. Too often what we see on social media creates an insecurity in ourselves, when those images do not tell the whole story. She believes this obsession with the next bandwagon gets us away from our why. Instead of getting caught up in teaching like someone else, Goldberg shows us the importance of teaching like ourselves.

—Peter DeWitt, Author and Consultant
Finding Common Ground Blog (*EdWeek*)

Gravity Goldberg understands the power of story! In Teach Like Yourself, *she urges us to find and use our core stories about teaching and learning to become more than a person who delivers a program or teaching script. She shares her personal accounts of when she practiced in ways that weren't true to herself, when she was [true to herself], and how she has learned to be more deeply attuned to her own authenticity, more often. She poses questions to help us explore how reflection, creativity, and imagination lead to responsive teaching and trusting relationships with students, colleagues, and ourselves. Each chapter moves us deeper into a process that puts us in touch with our core beliefs about teaching and learning and how to nurture and broaden those beliefs. Gravity shows us how to learn from students and other educators and take ownership of our teaching lives. Finally, her call to action—join the movement of #teachlikeyourself—invites us to transform the culture of accountability, teaching to tests, and blame into a culture that helps us find our teaching greatness.*

—Laura Robb, Education Consultant
Author, *Vocabulary Is Comprehension*

Teachers will find something precious in this deeply validating book from Gravity Goldberg: trust in themselves. Goldberg, using a mix of personal story and research, has given a gift to teachers, calling us to resist external pressures to compare and compete with each other and to listen to our own inner wisdom.

—Shanna Peeples, 2015 National Teacher of the Year
Author, *Think Like Socrates*

Gravity Goldberg reminds us all that successful teachers are driven less by curriculum guides and more by the relationships they take the time to build with colleagues, students, and families. Goldberg's personal stories give us more than a glimpse into her own continuous-improvement journey; in this way she builds an effective and instructive relationship with teachers at any grade level. I highly recommend this book for teachers and administrators.

—Ron Nash, Education Consultant
Author, *From Seatwork to Feetwork* and *The Active Classroom*

We often forget that to give our students the best, we need to be at our best. Gravity provides avenues within our practices and outside the classroom to rejuvenate our passion to teach authentically.

—Justin Stygles, Fifth-Grade Teacher
Wiscasset School Department

What I most love about Teach Like Yourself *is Goldberg's ability to focus on what really matters. A must-read for both experienced and novice teachers who are looking for a practical resource that gets to the heart of why we teach.*

—Carol Pelletier Radford
Author, *Mentoring in Action*
Founder, MentoringinAction.com

How I wish this book was out when I started teaching! The principles and strategies here will make me a better teacher even as a veteran. It is a gift to the field.

—Julie Stern, Author and Trainer

Like a spa day, reading Teach Like Yourself *affirms and pampers teachers' souls. Goldberg vividly pulls together personal stories, research-based practices, and reflection invitations into a gorgeous bouquet of support for teachers.*

—Kimberly Mitchell, Education Consultant at Inquiry Partners
Author, *Experience Inquiry*

Gravity Goldberg uses the term authentic teachers *to drive her mission of helping educators teach like themselves. With thoughtful reflection questions and powerful classroom examples, Goldberg places emphasis on students through the lens of authentic teaching and being true to oneself. This is a great choice for teachers, coaches, and school leaders at any stage of their career.*

—**Monica Burns,** Education Consultant
Author, #FormativeTech

Considering the current trend in teacher burnout, Teach Like Yourself *is a much-needed book that addresses "the whole teacher," and it does so by seamlessly intertwining stories, self-help strategies, research, and practical tips for the classroom. This book will serve as a much-needed shot in the arm for teachers who have lost their way, while helping all educators to enhance their work by encouraging them to be confident and stay true to who they are.*

—**Ross Cooper,** Principal
Author, *Hacking Project Based Learning*
T. Baldwin Demarast Elementary

Teach Like Yourself *is a priceless guide to help teachers to show up in the classroom every day as the most authentic version of themselves. This book guides teachers how to find their power within, rather than copying others in the classroom, leading to the all too common "imposter syndrome." Teaching like yourself and unlike anybody else is the most powerful way to present yourself in the classroom and for your students. This book is a perfect platform to build well-rounded, balanced, and happy teachers that can connect with the curriculum, students, and other teachers, as well as families.*

—**Serena Pariser,** Assistant Director of Field Experience
Author, *Real Talk About Classroom Management*
University of San Diego

Gravity Goldberg has written an inspirational book that will touch the heart and challenge the mind of educators who are looking for ways to meet the needs of their students. Not only does Gravity's work honor teachers' voice and agency but it instills a sense of hope and confidence in transforming learning and teaching in schools so that collective efficacy is realized.

—**Jenni Donohoo**, Consultant
Author, *Collective Efficacy*

Teachers don't need to be fixed; they need to be set free. Teach Like Yourself *gives practical insight to educators from all areas and grade levels. Gravity shares shifts that helped her teach like herself that everyone can relate to. Reading about her successes as well as her failures helps provide teachers with humble confidence and eliminate comparison teaching and self-doubt. Reading* Teach Like Yourself *will help you appreciate your strengths and create a highlight reel you'll want to replay over and over again. Teaching isn't easy, and Gravity shares just how to make the journey more smooth while enjoying it each step of the way. If you are still seeking to realize your "why" as an educator,* Teach Like Yourself *is for you.*

—**Kelsey Gavulic**, Student Teacher
Central Michigan University

As a first-year teacher, I've experienced so many of the feelings described in this book. Goldberg provides honest and real advice about how to work through the difficult times.

—**Megan Shofield**, Third-Grade Teacher
Wiscasset School Department

TEACH LIKE
YOURSELF

Dedicated to all the brave teachers who choose to show up fully as themselves each day.

TEACH LIKE YOURSELF

How Authentic Teaching
Transforms Our Students
and Ourselves

GRAVITY GOLDBERG

CORWIN
A SAGE Publishing Company

FOR INFORMATION:

Corwin

A SAGE Company

2455 Teller Road

Thousand Oaks, California 91320

(800) 233–9936

www.corwin.com

SAGE Publications Ltd.

1 Oliver's Yard

55 City Road

London, EC1Y 1SP

United Kingdom

SAGE Publications India Pvt. Ltd.

B 1/I 1 Mohan Cooperative Industrial Area

Mathura Road, New Delhi 110 044

India

SAGE Publications Asia-Pacific Pte. Ltd.

3 Church Street

#10–04 Samsung Hub

Singapore 049483

Acquisitions Editor: Ariel Curry

Development Editor: Desirée A. Bartlett

Editorial Assistant: Jessica Vidal

Production Editor: Tori Mirsadjadi

Copy Editor: Megan Markanich

Typesetter: Integra

Proofreader: Talia Greenberg

Indexer: Beth Nauman-Montana

Cover and Interior Designer: Janet Kiesel

Marketing Manager: Brian Grimm

Printed in the United States of America.

ISBN 978-1-5443-3735-7

This book is printed on acid-free paper.

SUSTAINABLE FORESTRY INITIATIVE

Certified Chain of Custody

Promoting Sustainable Forestry

www.sfiprogram.org

SFI-01268

SFI label applies to text stock

18 19 20 21 22 10 9 8 7 6 5 4 3 2 1

CONTENTS

CHAPTER 2:
NAME CORE BELIEFS

CHAPTER 3:
VIEW TEACHING AS A PRACTICE

CHAPTER 4:
BUILD BALANCED RELATIONSHIPS

CHAPTER 5:
DRIVE PROFESSIONAL GROWTH

CHAPTER 6:
TAKE CARE OF YOURSELF

CHAPTER 7:
TEACH BRAVELY

Note From the Publisher: The author has provided video and web content throughout the book that is available to you through QR (quick response) codes. To read a QR code, you must have a smartphone or tablet with a camera. We recommend that you download a QR code reader app that is made specifically for your phone or tablet brand. Videos may also be accessed at **http://resources.corwin.com/teachlikeyourself**

PREFACE

WHY I WROTE THIS BOOK

This is the fifth book I've published, and like every piece of writing, it begins with what Peter Elbow described as "an itch" to say something. With my other books, the itch was to help teachers confer, or improve independent reading, or cultivate student agency. What springs to mind for this project is that I wrote this book to cultivate *teacher* agency. Through teacher agency, student agency arrives as a happy by-product. I wrote this book to try to quell the teacher burnout I see all around. I wrote it imagining it as a graduation gift to new teachers; as a book to get early career teachers through rough times; and to help dispirited, seasoned teachers to reclaim their strength. I want every teacher to remain in the classroom and only leave the profession for all the right reasons. I want all teachers to feel passionately engaged and experience full ownership of how they teach. My goal is to help you to be authentically, fully "you" in the classroom—to teach like yourself, not like a robot, or a pirate, or a champion, or a superhero. You don't need those razzle-dazzle likenings. You just need you.

> You don't need those razzle-dazzle likenings. You just need you.

Unfortunately, in the United States 150,000 new teachers are trained each year, yet half of them quit within their first five years of teaching (Education International, 2017). While there is no single reason why early career teachers leave and experienced teachers feel burnout, a common theme that resonates with teachers is an overemphasis on accountability, standards, testing, and a narrative of mistrust of teachers' expertise. In addition, many teachers are in a crisis of confidence. Based on magazine articles I've read in recent months, news stories, conversations with educators, comments in social media, and the reported numbers of teachers downloading resources from Teachers Pay Teachers, I think it's fair to say that teachers nationwide are experiencing a profound loss of trust in themselves. There are many reasons for this lack of self-trust. A teacher may face roadblocks such as a lack of sound educational materials and curriculum or policies that get in the way of solid instruction. The net effect is self-doubt, a tendency to outsource decisions, and too many educators experiencing imposter syndrome. These trends can no longer be ignored, and I want to help.

Children are, by nature, empathic and can sense when a teacher is coming across as inauthentic and is playing a role due to burnout, pressure, lack of support, or fear of a new initiative. As a result, students may become anxious, guarded, or learn to play the game of school just to get by. We know that students learn more from teachers they trust and with whom they have a strong relationship. And students can't form strong relationships with teachers if they are not showing up as their true selves.

To stop this cycle, we teachers do not need fads, quick fixes, or magic bullet–style "kit" curriculum. Instead, we need a deep sense of self, a confidence in our practice, and the freedom to show up fully as ourselves. These "self-skills," if you will, are rarely addressed in preservice teacher education programs or professional development. While the confidence of any practitioner to some degree has to develop through experience, the concepts underlying the authentic self can be taught and ought to be taught in teacher education programs. Novice teachers enter the field with knowledge of standards, assessment, and lesson planning. While these basics are important, they are not enough to keep teachers engaged, happy, and motivated over the long haul. I envision an education system where every teacher feels prepared and empowered to teach like themselves, focusing on core values and living them day in, day out with their students.

ORGANIZATION OF THIS BOOK

This book is organized around five big ideas that both novice and veteran teachers can explore so that they can step fully into their roles as authentic teachers. Whether you are a new teacher trying to figure out who your authentic teacher self is or an experienced teacher who has seen the pendulum swing back and forth and is looking for some solid ground, this book is meant to help you. If I could, I would sit down with each of you, sip a cup of tea, and listen to your teaching story. What do you value? What successes have you experienced? What challenges keep you up at night? I would then share my stories—how I learned through both the good days and the very hard days of my teaching. What follows is a brief explanation of how I set up this book almost like a series of conversations. The book is divided into seven chapters, and next I explain what you might want to think about as you read each one.

Chapter 1 sets the foundation for what it means to teach like yourself and why authentic teaching is so important. I suggest you read this chapter asking yourself, "What does it mean to me to be an authentic teacher right now?"

Chapters 2 through 6 focus on five practices for teaching like yourself, and they comprise what I call the Teach Like Yourself Manifesto, which we'll go through in Chapter 7. These practices start with getting clear on your why (your core beliefs) and then aligning your why with your how. Your how entails your teaching practices, relationships, professional learning, and your self-care. These chapters help you consider how you can match your teaching to your own inner compass and not only survive but thrive as an authentic teacher. I suggest you read each of these chapters asking yourself the following questions:

- "What are my core beliefs about teaching?" (Chapter 2)

- "How can I align my teaching practices more fully to my core beliefs?" (Chapter 3)

- "How can I build stronger and more balanced relationships with my colleagues, students, and their families?" (Chapter 4)

- "In what ways can I drive my own professional growth and learning?" (Chapter 5)

- "How can I take care of my whole self, so I can show up healthy and ready to teach each day?" (Chapter 6)

Chapter 7 brings us back to the vital importance of authentic teaching and elaborates on the manifesto from the inside cover so you can teach like yourself each day. This chapter is a call to action to help you focus on what matters most. I suggest you ask yourself, "How can I choose to teach like myself each day, and how can I encourage my colleagues to do the same?"

THREE RECURRING FEATURES

Many of the books I read about teaching paint the rosiest picture, make the strategies seem easy to implement, or distill teaching down into steps and gimmicks. But real, honest, vulnerable teaching comes from a much deeper and messier place. I chose to include three main elements in the chapters that work in tandem to help you be your most authentic self. The three features are personal stories, research-based practices, and reflection sections for you to step back and consider the teacher you want to be.

Personal Stories

I could have cut out my personal stories and stuck to the research and reflection, but as a teacher I have seen how much we can learn from hearing each other's stories. Brené Brown (2015) writes, "When we deny our stories, they define us. When we own our stories, we get to write a brave new ending." She goes on to explain that owning our stories is standing in our truth. I couldn't write a truthful book about authentic teaching without sharing some of my mess-ups, traumas, and aha! moments. If you find yourself cringing at some of them, know that each of these moments was a major learning experience for me. In fact, I likely learned more from the uncomfortable parts of my teaching life than I did from the easy ones. I also included the stories of other teachers and administrators through video clips at the beginning of each chapter so we can learn from multiple educators' experiences. All of the videos can be viewed on the companion website at http://resources.corwin.com/teachlikeyourself.

I suggest you read these stories as teachable moments. See if you can find the common element in your own teaching experience. When I share a story of misjudging a colleague, think about the places and times when you may have done this too. When I share a story of connecting with a student, give yourself a few minutes to recall your similar experiences. I also suggest you look for the larger themes within the stories. Consider why I shared this story. You may ask yourself, "What did I take away from this story?" or "Where and why am I reacting to this story?" or "How can I learn from this story, without having to go through the exact same experience myself?"

Research-Based Practices

A second element of the chapters is research-based practices that come from education, leadership, and psychology. I included the research so that you understand the why behind the practices and also so you leave with some concrete ideas to go back and try. For example, in Chapter 4 I offer some research on how to cultivate strong, supportive, and balanced relationships with colleagues and include a list of what the research suggests. This list can serve as an anchor you can come back to as a proactive process of forming relationships or as a learning space for how to help shift a less-than-ideal relationship.

The research is always tied to some very practical tools, ideas, and experiences that I highlight in summary boxes. I suggest you pause after each summary box and take stock of what you already do as a teacher and what else you might try. I am confident that you will be reading about research that confirms what you already do. When this happens, smile, feel the confidence that fills you up, and remind yourself to keep doing that practice. You may also find some research that is different, new, or even contradictory to some of what you do as a teacher. When you encounter these places, I suggest you take time to consider if and how you may want to try out the new information. It doesn't hurt to try something new and see how it goes. I trust you to make shifts in manageable moves that will work for you and your students.

Invitations to Reflect

A third element of the book is reflection spaces for you to think, try something out, and then write about it right in the book. This is meant to be a safe space for you to not just read about a practice but to live it and write about what you discover. It is the space for you to write your teaching story and see it on the page. Once you write it down, you can make some choices: Do I want to share this with a mentor, colleague, or teaching partner? Do I want to make a major shift based on what I just wrote down? Do I see all the possibility that exists in my teaching, and can I capture that on the page? Can I see a more authentic version of my teacher self?

We know that being a reflective teacher is essential for growth and sustainability. Yet we often lack the time or support to sit and reflect on a regular basis. Give yourself the gift of time, and support yourself by reflecting on the questions and activities described in the book.

USE THE BOOK TO COACH YOURSELF

I think of this book as a sort of self-coaching tool. You can use it to take yourself on a journey into a deeper, more grounded, and even more satisfying career as a teacher. Coach Michael Bungay Stanier (2016) explains that "coaching should be a daily, informal act, not an occasional formal 'It's coaching time!' event" (p. 7). He also explains that "coaching can fuel the courage to step out beyond the comfortable and familiar, can help people learn from their experiences and can literally and metaphorically increase and help fulfill a person's potential" (p. 10). This doesn't mean you can't also work with a coach or mentor, as this is a wonderful opportunity, if you have one. It does mean that you can also coach yourself to fulfill your potential as a teacher. No one else knows what lies in your heart, what really motivated you to complete a teacher preparation program, and why you lay awake at night worrying about certain students. No one else knows what you say to yourself in your head as a lesson flops or shines. No one else knows what your authentic teaching self really looks like. As you read this book, please be patient and kind, taking it one practice at a time, allowing yourself the time and space to coach yourself more fully into a more authentic self.

ACKNOWLEDGMENTS

This book allowed me the space to make sense of my own teaching journey and to discover why it is that I have such deep passion and love for my life as an educator. In *The Courage to Teach*, Parker Palmer (1998) writes, "I am a teacher at heart, and there are moments in the classroom when I can hardly hold the joy.... But at other moments, the classroom is so lifeless or painful or confused... that my claim to be a teacher seems a transparent sham" (p. 1). I want to thank every teacher out there who has held that immense teacher joy and sat frozen in the pain. For me, being a teacher is deeply vulnerable, beautiful, and often challenging. It is in those challenging spaces—the moments between the utter joy and painful confusion—that this book arrived. I wrote this book with the help of every teacher, student, and colleague who entered my mind and my heart as each experience allowed me to reflect, learn, and grow into my true teacher self. For all of you, I am deeply grateful.

Teachers (whether you have that official job title or not) have been one of the most important gifts in my life. Thank you to John Altieri; Renee Houser; my mom, Josette Lumbruno; my dad, Gary Goldberg-O'Maxfield; Barbara McLaughlin; Carolyn Sullivan; Kathleen Flannery; Lucy Calkins; Kathleen Tolan; Kathy Collins; Laurie Pessah; Amanda Hartman; Karl Direske; Pat Miller; Bill Marple; Corrine Eisenmann; Dorothy Tremel; Donna Fairchild; Lanie Garner-Winter; Tim Grantham; Ann Hampton; Malini Mayherhouser; Brooke Geller; Patty McGee; Pam Koutrakos; Laura Sarsten; Karen Finnerty; Julie McAuley; Grace White; Gail Cordello; Chris Fuller; Sarah Fiedeldey; Kerrie Larosa; Matt Marone; Ross Cooper; Grace Oh; Joanie Miller; Carleigh Fairchild; Jen Stratton-Werry; Amanda Zabel; Zeb Browne; Ruth Bayer; Ben Weiss; Carol James; Justin Sutera; Mink Taylor; Seth Godin; Kelli Wood; Ian Scott; Julie Lifton; and Anodea Judith.

Thank you also to the team at Corwin who spend every day creating ways to support teachers. I am grateful for my editor, Ariel Curry, who conceived of and believed in this book and the core ideas behind it. Thank you to Wendy Murray, who edited my last four books and has become a friend and true thinking partner. The many dedicated members of Corwin helped this book become a reality—Lisa Luedeke, who found just the right title for this book because she is so gifted at knowing the authors she brings to Corwin; Janet Kiesel, who created this book's cover and interior design; Tori Mirsadjadi, who always makes sure each page is perfect; Desirée Bartlett and Jessica Vidal, who cross every T in a hundred ways in the course of making a book; and Julie Slattery and Cathy Hernandez, who distill many rambling video minutes into the telling few.

PUBLISHER'S ACKNOWLEDGMENTS

Corwin gratefully acknowledges the contributions of the following individual:

Dr. Kristen M. Ford, Chair, Health, Physical Education and Exercise Science Department
Associate Professor, Physical Education and Health Education Pedagogy
SchoolsAlive! Instructional Co-Designer and Trainer
Concordia College
Moorhead, MN

AUTHENTIC
TEACHING

Video 1

To read a QR code, you must have a smartphone or tablet with a camera. We recommend that you download a QR code reader app that is made specifically for your phone or tablet brand. Videos may also be accessed at http://resources.corwin.com/teachlikeyourself

Source: One 21 Production

If you can see your path laid out in front of you step by step, you know it's not your path. Your own path you make with every step you take. That's why it's your path.

—Joseph Campbell

Right now I am pregnant with my first baby. I am at a threshold, not quite leaving my old identity behind but about to take on a new one. I will no longer just be Gravity or Dr. Goldberg, but I will also be known as Mom. This has brought along excitement and fear of the unknown, fear of losing myself, and fear of not being quite good enough. One of the last times I felt this way, standing at a major life threshold, was when I became a teacher. One day I was a twenty-one-year-old college student who had spent my whole life known as Gravity, and a few months later I was walking into my own classroom where I would be known as Ms. Goldberg. I was excited about finally being in my classroom, and I eagerly anticipated meeting my new students. But I was also terrified I would not be good enough and everyone would realize I was a fraud, not quite ready to have these humans under my guidance and care each day.

What feels strangely similar between becoming a mom and a teacher are the ways others have attempted to support me during this transition. As a new teacher, my colleagues all wanted to give me advice: "Don't smile until November"; and "Don't let your papers pile up, do a little grading each day"; and "When the principal comes in to observe you, stick to what you do well. Don't take any risks." They meant well and wanted to see me succeed. Likely most of this advice had been handed down to them from their more experienced teacher friends. As a soon-to-be mom, everyone has advice too. "Take the epidural," and "Don't let that baby into your bedroom or you will never get them out," and "Puree your own food so your baby doesn't wind up living on mac and cheese and chicken nuggets as a toddler." Do you remember all of the advice you received as a new teacher? Or maybe you're in your first year and getting unsolicited advice all of the time.

During a recent phone conversation with my aunt she gave me the best advice so far. She offered, "**Trust your instincts.** You will know what is right for your baby. Don't overthink it. And don't take everyone's advice. **Listen to yourself.**" If I were to go back and meet my first-year teacher self, I would steal my aunt's words and tell them to myself daily. "Trust your instincts. You will know what is right for your students. Don't overthink it. Listen to yourself." In many ways, this book is a longer version of this advice I wish I could go back and offer myself and the advice I want you to have for yourself. It took some time for me to realize that being my true self as a teacher was exactly what my students needed. But it turned out that figuring out who my true teacher self was required lots of reflection and searching. What took even longer was my journey to actually living the practices of my authentic teacher self with all of my students. I had to take time to really own it. I want teachers to take less time than I did to get there.

> Being your true self as a teacher is exactly what your students need.

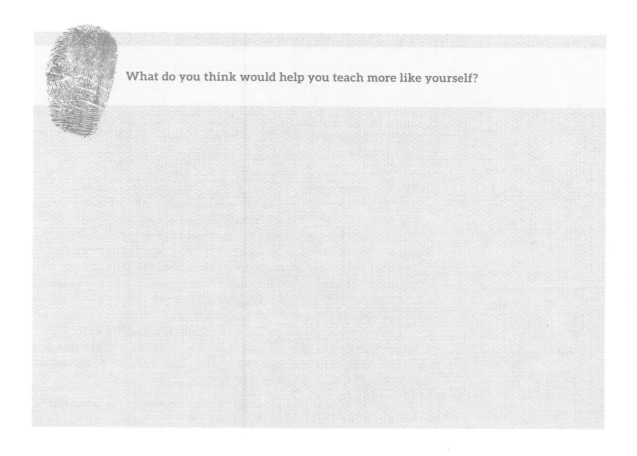

What do you think would help you teach more like yourself?

WHAT HELPS US BE AUTHENTIC TEACHERS?

Over the past two decades I have served as a science teacher, reading specialist, third-grade teacher, special educator, literacy coach, staff developer, assistant professor, consultant, and yoga teacher. This means I have taught students from age four through eighty. Each and every teaching opportunity helped me refine and define what it means for me to teach like myself, to take my aunt's advice, and to bring my best and most authentic self to each set of students. What I realized is that my specific teaching assignment and my students would often change, but the one constant was me and how I chose to show up as a teacher.

Remember That There Is Nothing to Fix

For several decades, people have been obsessed with self-help books that popularized the research and theories of the medical and psychology fields. The problem was, it grew out of a 20th century problem-oriented paradigm that focused on curing illness, disease, and deficits. The self-help movement that arose operated on the assumption that there is something wrong with you that you need to get help from outsiders to fix. Frankly, that whole idea always left me depleted, beaten down, and feeling insecure about myself.

Fortuitously, we are now in the heyday of a happiness movement. It started about twenty years ago when Martin Seligman championed a new branch of psychology that, studies what makes humans thrive—positive psychology. In 1990, *Flow: The Science of Optimal Experience* by Mihaly Csikszentmihalyi was published in the United States, and it quickly became a bestseller. The so-called science of happiness hit the mainstream with that book, and if you haven't read it, I suggest you do. Other popular books, such as *Learned Optimism* by Martin Seligman (2006), *The Happiness Advantage* by Shawn Achor (2010), and *The Happiness Project* by Gretchen Rubin (2015), suggest that the tide has turned, and the self-help movement has evolved into one of self-acceptance and self-discovery, which feels entirely different. This new movement assumes you are already awesome, with many unique talents and quirks that make you, you. Instead of anything needing to be fixed, the idea is to accept and embrace yourself and to build from your strengths. Most of the people I know feel much more motivated when they start from ownership rather than feeling like there is something wrong.

> Most of the people I know feel much more motivated when they start from ownership rather than feeling like there is something wrong.

In the field of education, however, I think we are too often operating in the old-think of the problem-based self-help movement. Coming at us from every direction are blog posts, articles, in-service providers, workshops, and even op-ed pieces that offer teachers steps and strategies that will "fix" something that is wrong with your teaching. If anyone is approaching us teachers as in need of being fixed, I end up walking out the door or closing the book because this person assumes there is something wrong. This person who never met me or my students and never stepped into my classroom thinks she can solve a problem I have not yet even articulated. This doesn't mean we shy away from coaching and mentoring. As teachers, we can constantly learn from those who approach us from a strength-based model. The teacher community does not need one more teacher-help resource that assumes we lack something or that something about our practice needs to be fixed. Instead, we need the equivalent to the teacher-acceptance and discovery model. There are, of course, many workshops and professional books that don't assume we need to be fixed and instead treat us like professionals with much to offer and build upon to strengthen our practice. Those are the books that line my bookshelf with sticky notes and highlights.

As I sit down to write this book, I assume you are already a talented educator and there is nothing I need to help you fix. You are in teaching for a reason. You're here not only because a university or teacher prep program gave you a degree; most importantly, you're here because you believe that you are supposed to be here. I do think that a bit of self-discovery and ways to consciously build from our strengths as teachers is really helpful—at least it has been for me. This means we all can grow in our teaching practice and view each day as a learning opportunity—not from a place of insecurity but instead from a place of humble confidence. We must know our strengths so well that we can leverage them and bring our best, most authentic self to our students. This book will help you discover the unique strengths and talents that you bring to the profession and, most importantly, to your students.

> You're here because you believe that you are supposed to be here.

Stop Comparing Ourselves to Someone Else's Highlight Reel

Many of us feel the need to fix something or change something about our teaching when we look at others and make comparisons. When I compare myself to others, I tend to paint them in the rosiest light and see only their strengths. But when it comes to me—I am the toughest critic. I focus only on my perceived faults. I have found I am not alone in this comparison game. Many teacher friends have admitted they torture themselves by comparing themselves (almost always negatively) to their peers and mentors. Of course, most books, coaches, and conferences highlight the positive practices and leave out the terrifying challenges that led to that success.

Nothing epitomizes this more than Pinterest and my preferred favorite: Pinterest fails. Pinterest posts show us perfection in just a few easy steps. My feed is often filled with pins like "10 Minutes to Washboard Abs" and "Pumpkin Baby Photo Shoot," featuring a photo of a smiling infant stuffed inside a carved-out pumpkin with her legs and arms hanging out of tiny holes. Of course, I have never met anyone who worked out only ten minutes a day and had washboard abs. And the "fails" photo shows the reality: a baby crying hysterically and trying to get out of an ill-carved pumpkin, red-faced with snot running down her nose. No one posts or pins the thousands of attempts that were messy failures prior to the one lucky example the camera caught. Those Pinterest lessons seem so perfect on the screen but almost always fall flat and miss the mark with our students. It is easy to compare and then feel bad about ourselves, leading us back to thinking we need to be fixed.

I learned I didn't need to do so much comparing from one of my mentors at the Teachers College Reading and Writing Project, Kathy Collins. This totally smart, funny, and talented educator shared her challenges and faults with us. She would move back and forth between self-deprecating stories of some big failure to teaching us a remarkable way to work with primary-grade readers. She helped me embrace and acknowledge the parts of teaching and learning that are most often left out of our conversations. The fact is, lessons and ideas almost never work out the first time, and we almost all fail several times before we succeed. By bringing all of this into her workshops, Kathy modeled for me what it sounds like, looks like, and feels like to show up as her true self. Because Kathy was sharing all her experiences, not just the Pinterest-worthy ones, with us, I realized that the comparisons I tended to make were based on half-truths. It wasn't fair to me or my teaching to compare all of myself to someone else's highlight reel.

As her student, I trusted her and wanted to soak up every moment of learning with her because she was so human. She took risks, laughed at herself, was thoughtful and reflective, and viewed each moment as a chance to learn more. The more Kathy was herself, the more I could show up as myself too. Because I didn't just see her highlight reel, I could see how she refined her practice, considered alternatives, and carried a growth mindset into her work. I could do the same.

This pattern proves true no matter the age of the students. When I watched Kathy teach first graders, they hung on her every word, took risks in their learning, and spent time sharing reflections with their first-grade partners. It was remarkable how much these five- and six-year-olds were able to do because of Kathy's modeling. When teaching a reading mini lesson, she didn't make her reading look easy or magical; she made it look real. She showed how she worked hard and tried a few strategies. I saw student after student go back to their seats and have the confidence to try strategies themselves because they were not comparing themselves to a magical reading lesson but instead to an authentic one.

Focus on What We Can Control

When we teachers walk into classrooms as ourselves and share our stories, our learning process—warts and all—it gives permission for our students to do the same. When we silence our challenges, hide them from our students, and play the "teacher role" it sends the message that students should play the "student role." Then we are all playing school instead of digging into the learning.

"Doing school" (Pope, 2003) refers to the commonly expressed experience of high schoolers who see school as a game that must be played. The students focus on how to get the best grade, get teachers to like them, and then get into the best colleges. In his book *Excellent Sheep,* William Deresiewicz (2014) explains how common it is for college freshmen in elite colleges to suffer from anxiety, depression, and self-destructive behaviors as a result of doing school and feeling pressure to be perfect. Further, Dr. Peter Gray cites research by Twenge and colleagues (2010) that students today are more likely to suffer from anxiety and depression than previous generations of kids due to a decline in students' sense of personal control over their fates and shifts toward extrinsic goals and away from intrinsic goals. Gray (2010) states, "Intrinsic goals are those that have to do with one's own development as a person—such as becoming competent in endeavors of one's choosing and developing a meaningful philosophy of life. Extrinsic goals, on the other hand, are those that have to do with material rewards and other people's judgments."

Put in the context of doing school, many students today feel pressure to fit the ideal and make the grades (extrinsic goals) and are consumed with fears of failure or perceived failure by others. Gray (2010) explains, "To the extent that my emotional sense of satisfaction comes from progress toward intrinsic goals, I can control my emotional well-being. To the extent that my satisfaction comes from others' judgments and rewards, I have much less control over my emotional state." The theory of Twenge and colleagues (2010) is that when people feel they have no control over their lives and how they are measured, it can lead to anxiety and depression. When our brains are anxious and depressed, we cannot fully show up as ourselves, and we cannot be fully present to learn.

As a teacher, when I focus too much on external goals—evaluations, test scores, and formal observation feedback—I become anxious. My brain swims with "what-ifs" such as these: What if this lesson is not good enough? What if I didn't do a good enough job preparing my students? These what-ifs can send me spinning down a rabbit hole of trying to control everything in the classroom. This controlling mode takes me out of myself, and I end up playing the teacher role that I think the external evaluator will approve of. It is totally and utterly exhausting to try to control 20 to 100 students a day, how they will respond to my lessons, and how outsiders visiting my classroom will perceive and judge it. The truth is, I actually have no control over others, and it wastes my time and energy to focus my attention there.

What I've found is that the more I focus on my own definition of success and my intrinsic goals for my students, the better it works out for everyone. For example, if my goal for students is for them to use many strategies we have learned and apply them to a complex, multistep problem without giving up, I beam with pride after a few days of seeing this in action. Or if I set a goal for myself to sit side by side and get to know each student in my writing class as individuals, at the end of the week I can reflect with satisfaction on my accomplishment—knowing my students a little better than the week before. These intrinsic goals are set by me and evaluated by me. In reality, the only thing I have control over are my own intrinsic goals and the choices I make toward them. When I model this for my students, we all learn the importance of our own locus of control and we combat the anxiety-producing "doing school" behaviors. Where are you placing your locus of control?

Share Our Gifts and Talents

When I graduated from Boston College with a teaching degree, I was eager to be just like the teachers I admired. I had sixteen years' worth of their influence, and I believed I could take the best of each of them and become a hybrid version. I would inspire like my twelfth-grade English teacher, I would build student curiosity like my third-grade teacher, and I would have high expectations like my student teaching cooperating teacher. I believed I could sort of paste them together to form my own teaching identity. While it is totally natural and helpful to lean heavily on mentors in our early teaching days and to remember that experience is the best teacher, nowhere in that plan did I consider what *I* believed and what *I* could offer as my own gifts and talents.

During the first few years of my teaching I was like many new teachers, walking the line between excitement and fear. I was excited to try a new lesson or method and see what my students did. I was also terrified I was not good enough and that I was not doing what my students really needed. There were more fears, too, if I am totally honest. Did my principal like me, and did she think I was doing a good job? Did my students like me, and did they leave each day wanting to come back the next one? Did I know enough about math or science to teach it well? Was it my fault that some students just didn't get what I was teaching? Should I ask for more help from my grade-level peers, or was I already asking too much of them? The list could go on and on. I guess another line I was walking was between confidence and self-doubt. I cried on some days and met friends out for drinks on good days when I wanted to celebrate.

I did reflect a lot, usually with friends on long phone calls or in journal entries. Much of what I realized was that the days I cried, I almost always second-guessed myself and did something I knew just didn't feel right. These were the lessons I tried to copy from someone else or when I tried to be someone else. I tried to be funny like Deb, or serious like Tom, or perfectly put together like Mary. These colleagues of mine were funny, serious, put together, and great teachers, but they were not me. It never really worked to try to be anyone else as a teacher. At the time, I didn't believe I could just be me, and I didn't understand really what that even meant. The stories that follow illustrate how things changed for me and my students when I learned to be more of myself in the classroom. See if any of these stories resonate with your experiences, feelings, and insecurities as a teacher.

During my second teaching year, I taught third grade to an extremely energetic and diverse group of students. I was learning a new phonics program and using the teacher's manual to help me. I held up phonics cards for my students to read aloud, I read a sentence for dictation as they wrote it on their papers, and then I guided them with the exact prompts from the manual to code the spelling patterns in each word. I got halfway through the dictation portion when I noticed several students stopped working. I got annoyed and told them to pick their pencils up and start writing. Even my "best student" just stared at me. Finally I asked, "Why aren't you writing?" One boy spoke up and said, "It doesn't make any sense. What are you talking about?" I looked at their papers to see what they had written so far and realized I left out key words and inserted a word so that the sentence made absolutely no sense. I hadn't even been listening to what I was saying, and instead, I just read what was written in my plans. My face turned red, and I apologized to my class. That night I decided I was going to use the program as a guide, but I was going to write my own sentences for dictation. The ones given to me just felt so disconnected from me and my students. I wanted them to write about topics they cared about and I could talk about. This one change made all the difference. Students looked forward to hearing the sentence each day and then discussing what it meant and why I chose it. It became a puzzle for them to solve rather than a mindless activity to survive.

During my third year of teaching, I was so psyched about teaching writing workshop. It was my favorite part of the day, and I spent the most time planning and preparing for each day's lesson. I wrote daily in my own writing notebook, modeled strategies, and spent time sitting side by side with students having conferences and giving them feedback on their writing. I showed my vulnerability to my students by making my writing process visible, by explaining how I struggled to come up with ideas, how I second-guessed my decisions, and how I tended to write about what felt safe and easy at first. I showed them an entry in my writing notebook about how great my cat was (a safe and boring entry) and then how I pushed myself to write with more honesty about the time I had to say goodbye to my dying dog (a risky, real, and raw entry). That year, my students groaned when the writing period ended and asked if they could take their writing notebooks to recess to keep writing. Really … they wanted to write at recess. The athlete in me said no and explained that they needed to run around and play too. But I knew something was working when it came to my writing instruction.

My principal observed a writing lesson, and in our debrief meeting she commented, "You really bring yourself into your writing lessons. You show your students what you do and how you do it. They hang on your every word." I nodded in thanks for her positive observation. Then she said, "What if you brought that level of ownership into your math teaching too?" That brief "praise high" faded as I realized she was right. At that time, my math lessons were uninspired. I simply went through the motions of what I had seen my colleagues do, my own math teachers, and what I thought a math lesson was supposed to look like. She followed up by asking, "If you could teach math the way *you* wanted, what would it look like?" I responded without even thinking, "It would look like the way I teach writing." She smiled and said, "Then go do that." What my principal knew was that I was still learning that the best teaching and learning come from having ownership.

Later in my career, while serving as a coach to teachers, I met a fourth-year middle school teacher, Barb, who requested support in her classroom. She met with me to discuss what she wanted to work on. Barb explained that she inherited her curriculum, liked some of the units she was supposed to teach, but that she found many of the lessons and assessments burdensome and frankly not that connected to her own vision of what she wanted her classroom to be like. She wanted to make some changes but was afraid of what her more experienced colleagues would say. Barb and I planned some shifts she wanted to make and I pushed into her classroom to model lessons, co-teach, and then coach her as she tried the new moves. She began to feel excited and could see how these shifts were positively affecting her students. But ... Barb was still afraid to share her new ideas at the department meetings. She worried she would "be in trouble" with her colleagues for not using the workbook they passed down to her.

Barb and I made a plan to collaboratively share how the changes helped her students. We brought student work samples and showed our colleagues how much students were learning. When they asked how this happened, I smiled at Barb, and she explained some of the new things she was trying out. Instead of being angry, her much more experienced colleagues asked if they could hear more and come into her classroom to see how it was going. Barb was beaming when she left the room. I simply said to her, "Because you were willing to take a risk and teach like yourself and not just teach like your colleagues, you modeled for your team how they can teach more like themselves." The truth is, even with years and years of experience, we all can benefit from reminders of being true to our own teacher selves.

The best teaching and learning come from having ownership.

The truth is, even with years and years of experience, we all can benefit from reminders of being true to our own teacher selves.

What Helps Us Be Authentic Teachers?

★ Remember that there is nothing to fix.

★ Stop comparing ourselves to someone else's highlight reel.

★ Focus on what we can control.

★ Share our gifts and talents.

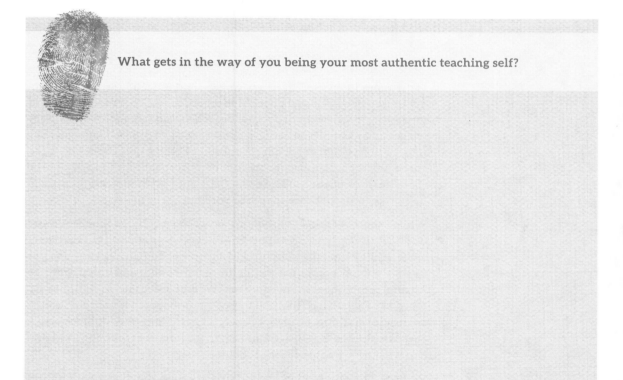

What gets in the way of you being your most authentic teaching self?

SHIFTS THAT HELP US TEACH MORE LIKE OURSELVES

While everyone—you, your students, and your colleagues—benefit from you teaching like yourself, it can be really hard. I've had many days when I felt like an imposter and second-guessed myself. I have copied other people's lessons. I have done something just because my colleagues were doing it, even when I didn't believe in it. A good portion of learning to teach like yourself is the trial and error that time and experience bring. That being said, I found three main challenges on my own journey to owning my teaching:

- Thinking I needed to entertain my students

- Changing the way I predict student outcomes

- Blaming students rather than acknowledging my role

I'll share a few stories that show what I learned from each of these fairly common challenges and offer you space to reflect on your own challenges.

From Being Interesting to Being Interested

Many times in my early teaching career—and, if I am honest, later on in my career too—I believed I needed to entertain my students and be super interesting. I believed I had to use gimmicks and talk fast or show crazy images and examples to capture my students' attention. I thought they wanted to be entertained. On my most energetic days I could pull it off, but it was totally unsustainable to entertain students all day long. The older the ages of my students, the harder it became to entertain them too. I was confusing entertainment with engagement.

While I could get and keep students' attention for a good fifteen minutes if I showed a crazy science video or I told a shocking story, it didn't actually mean my students were engaged in any meaningful learning. I began to shift my focus from me having to be interesting and entertaining to becoming interested in my students. When I asked them questions, listened closely to what they had to say, and followed a bit of their lead, it changed everything. I had more energy. I got to know my students better. Students showed up engaged and eager to show me what they could do and what they wanted to learn about.

While teaching in a self-contained special education class, I had so much trouble getting every student's attention (and there were only seven of them). So, I began sitting side by side with students. When I sat down next to a student that first morning, I didn't even know why I did, but I was trusting my instinct. I asked the student, and then the others, what they knew a lot about and what they could be teachers about. I was about to start a unit on teaching students how to write informational books, and rather than focus on the content, at first I decided to focus on being genuinely interested in my students. As I had conversations with each student, I learned that Myles was obsessed with Batman and that Juan knew so much about an animal called a Gila monster. The next

A good portion of learning to teach like yourself is the trial and error that time and experience bring.

day, when I began teaching students how to plan out an informational book by making a table of contents, I modeled with a topic I cared deeply about: running. Then I asked students to create their own table of contents about the topic they cared and knew the most about. As the days went by and students drafted their books, I modeled strategies for writing, but equally important, I asked a lot of genuinely curious questions I had about their topics and their writing. Every time I got curious about my students, their level of engagement rose, and I ended up feeling more energized and less depleted than the days of thinking I needed to entertain my students all day long. The truth I learned from this challenge is that true engagement comes from being interested in our students, not from providing them entertainment.

From Predicting Failure to Building on Success

A common, not so helpful habit I used to be stuck in was predicting what would happen in a lesson and what my students would not be able to do. Whenever I went into predicting mode, I stressed myself out and usually underestimated my students. The same is true for my colleagues. If I predicted how they would react to a new idea I wanted to share, it would usually psych me out from actually sharing it. My habit, I found out from other teachers, is quite common. It goes like this:

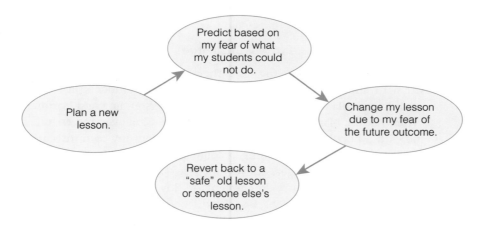

The real impact of this predicting habit was that I was often not that accurate in my ability to predict the future. With all the gifts I have, future-telling is not one of them. I think this is due to my fear of the messiness of the learning getting in the way of trying out something new. When in doubt (which was often), I ended up predicting my students would not be able to do it, and I played it safe.

Psychologists call this the Pygmalion effect (Achor, 2010), when our teacher expectations affect actual student learning. From several studies, we know that when teachers believe their students can achieve, their students will rise to the challenge, and when teachers set much lower expectations and believe their students cannot do something, students only meet those lower expectations. Basically, what we believe about our students ends up coming true. While at first this finding can be a bit scary—we have so much power—it can also feel like a long, deep breath. If we predict our students can learn something new and challenging, it is much more likely to happen.

I began to shift my planning away from predicting and instead focused on what my students could already do that I could build upon. I would begin my planning by looking at student work and naming what they were learning to do. For example, I noticed that many students could accurately read math problems with more than one part and that they could choose a mathematical operation that matched the problem. They had strengths I could build upon to plan the next steps of computing correctly and double-checking work. This felt good and much better than the negative predictions. Then I asked myself, "What is the next step these students are ready for?" By building from strengths, I was still making a prediction of sorts, but it was what they were ready for and it was based on their actual current work. This shift made me happier, helped me appropriately challenge my students, and led to much more student growth.

From Their Challenge to My Challenge

This shift is a difficult one to admit. There were several times as a teacher when I found myself saying something like, "My students just don't get it." I was blaming my students for not understanding and learning. When I began blaming, it was like a tidal wave took over and engulfed me with a hopeless feeling. It often stemmed from my own insecurity about my knowledge or teaching. It could also turn into the blame game where I could point fingers at everyone else out of pure frustration and think, "The parents don't do enough" or "My colleagues gave me the tough class." When I look back at these beliefs, I cringe and want to run and hide from shame. Often, I would go into blaming mode when I felt pressure to meet an expectation or when I was disappointed in how a lesson or experience went. At first it was easier to look outside myself than to take some personal responsibility for what I could have done differently. It took some honest reflection and time to realize that blaming was not helping anyone.

The times in my life when I was blamed for something, I shut down, got defensive, and disconnected from the person pointing the finger.

These are the same behaviors I saw in my students and my colleagues when they felt they were being blamed. Blaming makes someone the enemy and creates a chasm in the relationship. It also leads to mistrust. Authentic learning and relationships cannot flourish in an environment where people shut down and disconnect.

In some cases, students accept the blame and then take on a negative identity. I've seen it with a class of seventh graders who were sadly labeled as *low* and how they took on the identity and then sat passively in class waiting for a teacher to do the work for them. The self-blame can lead to low self-confidence and a fixed mindset. On the other hand, when no one is blaming themselves or the others in the school community, each person can develop a healthy identity with a growth mindset.

One experience as a graduate student really helped to shift my thinking about blame. I was taking a really hard class that involved lots of reading and research. I bombed my first few assignments and went in for extra help. Instead of offering tips or teaching, the professor began blaming me for being too busy teaching to focus on my coursework. I couldn't even get a question out of my mouth because she was talking at me with her mind made up. I went home and looked carefully at the midterm exam and realized that at least one third of the questions were on topics we did not even discuss in class. The irony, of course, was that this was an educational methods course, and she was not modeling what she was having us read about. Many of the readings advanced research and theories about student-centered curriculum, yet it was clear that she was more invested in the content than in getting to know us students. I was doing all of my readings, meeting with friends to study, and putting in so much effort.

One night, while talking (really, venting) to a nonteacher friend, she offered these questions to me: "Is it your problem or your professor's? Who is really struggling?" I answered, "I think she is. Or at least we both are. When I talk to the other students, we are all so confused, and no one is doing well." This conversation led me to stay up all night thinking about my own classroom and my own teaching.

Whenever I blamed my students or their parents for not doing their part or not understanding or not putting the work in, I could be looking back at myself instead. What was I doing to address the challenge? After more reflection, I realized that all those lessons that students did not understand were really the part of the curriculum that I did not know how to teach well. I was confusing where the real challenge was—it was often in my own teaching and not just in my students' learning. I learned that whenever my students are struggling, it does not help anyone to start

> Authentic learning and relationships cannot flourish in an environment where people shut down and disconnect.

blaming, and instead, I now begin looking at my own teaching practice to see what the real challenge is for me. Identifying and owning it as my challenge allows me to do something about it. Teaching like yourself doesn't excuse us from taking responsibility; it actually means taking more personal responsibility for what happens in our classrooms.

> Teaching like yourself doesn't excuse us from taking responsibility; it actually means taking more personal responsibility for what happens in our classrooms.

Shifts That Can Help Us Teach More Like Ourselves

★ Be genuinely curious and interested in our students instead of trying to gain their interest with entertaining teaching.

★ Build from students' current strengths with high expectations, rather than predicting what they would not be able to do.

★ Take responsibility for our own teaching challenges, rather than blame our students, their parents, or our colleagues.

What shifts might help you teach more like yourself?

FIVE PRACTICES FOR TEACHING LIKE YOURSELF

Writing a book about teaching like yourself is a challenge because I can't simply tell you what I did and suggest you do the same. That would really be missing the whole point of being your true self. So I can't offer you steps or tips. What I can offer are the practices I have witnessed in myself and countless other teachers as we've come to really own their teaching in truly powerful ways. What follows is a brief description about each practice. Know that each practice also has its own chapter, with examples and ideas to help you step more fully into teaching like yourself, and is part of the larger Teach Like Yourself Manifesto (see Chapter 7). Think of this like a sneak peek.

Name Your Core Beliefs

Part of being yourself is naming and knowing your own core beliefs about teaching and learning. By naming these beliefs, we create our framework and foundation to which we can come back over and over again. This feels like the heart of our teaching. Every other choice we make stems from the beliefs just like all our organs are fed from the blood that pumps through our hearts. By writing down our beliefs, we can revisit them, remind ourselves of them, and revise them as we gain more and more experience with students.

View Your Teaching as a Practice

Another part of teaching like yourself is connecting your teaching to your beliefs. This means examining teaching choices to see whether they match what we want for our students and what we value. By viewing our teaching as a practice, we can adjust, change course, and rethink our teaching choices on an ongoing basis. We can see that each class, each student interaction, and each lesson offers an opportunity to craft our practice. Doctors have a medical practice and lawyers have a law practice; really, everyone hones their craft, from carpenters to hair stylists, and we teachers can do the same. The term *practice* also reminds us that we have never learned it all or arrived at perfection but always have more to learn and develop.

> We have never learned it all or arrived at perfection but always have more to learn and develop.

Build Balanced Relationships

Teaching like yourself doesn't mean shutting your classroom door and becoming an island. It actually means cultivating the kinds of professional relationships that nurture and sustain you. When we begin to take the risks to be ourselves as teachers, it gives our colleagues permission to do the same. After all, none of us can have any true and lasting relationships with each other when we are all pretending to be something we are not. The same goes for our student relationships. According to the Quaglia Student Voice Survey (2016), students who have a sense of purpose, believe they can be successful, and are supported by their teachers are seventeen times more academically motivated. Students learn more and better from teachers they like and connect with. Teacher credibility, an outcome of student and teacher relationships, is one of John Hattie's (2016) top qualities for effective instruction with a 0.9 effect size. By building strong, real relationships with everyone in our schools, we are more at ease, more effective, and frankly have much more fun.

Drive Professional Growth

Teaching like yourself does not mean being stagnant and stopping your learning. It actually means the opposite. When we know ourselves well—our strengths, our blind spots, and our insecure parts—we can begin to seek professional opportunities that will help us grow. This used to mean signing up for workshops. While I am still a huge fan of workshops, we don't always get permission from administrators to leave the building or there may not be a budget. We can also seek professional growth opportunities for free or next to nothing. Getting on Twitter and joining professional chats, viewing webinars, and reading blog posts and articles are all great ways to develop in an area you want to learn more about. Reading professional books with colleagues in book clubs is a way to both build relationships and develop and grow. In fact, there are so many learning opportunities for teachers today, the challenge is choosing what you want to focus on.

There are so many learning opportunities for teachers today, the challenge is choosing what you want to focus on.

Take Care of Yourself

This final practice is much more than just being yourself as a teacher; it is about making sure you are taking care of your whole self so you can show up healthy, happy, and ready to teach. So many teachers I know (including myself at times) run themselves down, skip lunch, don't get to go to the bathroom, and respond to e-mails late into the evening. We stay up too late. We have trouble saying no. We put ourselves last. As teachers, we are not just modeling how to read, or solve math problems, or synthesize historical events; we are also modeling how to take care of ourselves. Plus, when we get sick or exhausted all those other intentional practices go out the window. We take shortcuts because we can't possibly handle being our best selves. Getting fresh air, drinking enough water, saying no to things you can't possibly handle, and creating healthy boundaries are all a part of teaching like yourself too.

Five Practices for Teaching Like Yourself

★ Name your core beliefs.

★ View your teaching as a practice.

★ Build balanced relationships.

★ Drive professional growth.

★ Take care of yourself.

Look at the description of the five practices for teaching like yourself. Which one stands out to you the most? Why? Which do you think you already do well? Which are you excited to learn more about?

As this chapter ends, I'll remind us of that helpful advice from my aunt: Trust yourself. You will know what is right. Listen to your instincts. In Chapter 2, we'll dive into the practices that will help us do exactly that—let's begin by naming our core beliefs.

NAME
CORE BELIEFS

Video 2

Source: One 21 Production

You will always belong anywhere you show up as yourself and talk about yourself and your work in a real way.

—Brené Brown

I realized I was afraid of heights in high school during an Outward Bound experience. I quickly and eagerly climbed up the rope ladder to the top of the trees, but when I looked down, I froze in fear. I was harnessed in and there was no way I could get injured, yet my mind did not believe reality and I cried and shook until I was literally pulled down by the guide. Since then, I realized my fear was not of going up high but of falling. I know this is ironic, since my name is Gravity. What scares me is plummeting down to injury or worse. For years, I told my friends and family that I wanted to conquer this fear, and my husband, John, was listening.

One year for Christmas, my husband thoughtfully gave me the gift of a trapeze lesson to do something "fun" to face my fear. So during the last days of summer (a good six months after the gift was given), I drove to trapeze school and signed up for the lesson. After the perfunctory safety lecture, I watched a ten-year-old boy volunteer to go first. He sprinted up the ladder, grabbed ahold of the trapeze handle, and took off in flight. It looked so easy. When it was my turn to be fastened into the harness and climb the ladder, I shook and trembled. My body did not believe what my mind was trying to tell it: "You will be fine. It will be fun."

I got to the top of the ladder and stepped onto the tiny platform. I did not look down. Instead, I decided to look out, and this is when it hit me that I was not only several feet in the air on a trapeze platform but I was also four stories in the air on the roof of a building where the apparatus was stationed. I was higher than many of the apartment buildings in the area and taller than any trees in sight. I took several long, deep breaths. The instructor told me to walk to the edge of the platform, and as I did this, she grabbed the back of my harness and pulled me tightly. "Now reach out and grab the bar," she explained. In order to grab the bar, I would need to go on my tip toes and lean over the edge. The only thing keeping me from falling from the platform was the hand holding on to the back of my harness. She had to repeat her directions. "You are not going to let go, are you?" I pleaded. She responded, "Not until you say go."

I stood on one foot's toes and then the other and reached out to grab the bar. My sweaty palms stuck, and I stopped holding my breath. "Now count to three and then say go," the instructor reminded me. I nodded that I understood and hoped my body would cooperate. "Remember, you have to jump out or you will not get any swing. If you just drop, you won't get any momentum," she said with years of experience behind her.

"Jump?" I thought to myself. "It is not enough to just let go and swing, I have to jump!" I began to count out loud, "One, two, three, GO!" On the word *go*, I did just that—I bent my knees and pushed off the platform and jumped up a good few feet before feeling the wind at my face from flying through the air. I swung and smiled and screamed. And I ended up getting several more trips on the trapeze, each one just as terrifyingly fun.

There were many moments during that trapeze day when I asked myself hard questions such as "Will I survive?" and "Am I brave enough to do this?," but I never asked myself this question: "Why am I doing this?" I didn't have to ask this question because I got crystal clear on my purpose months before I signed up for the class—I wanted to enjoy heights, and I no longer wanted to be afraid of falling. My clear purpose is what helped propel me off that platform. I would not have even been on that trapeze if I didn't have such a core belief about why it was important.

START WITH WHY

Simon Sinek's (2009) research and best-selling book explain that typical leaders begin by telling you *what* to do, then *how* to do it, and maybe include *why* at the end. But the most authentic and effective leaders start with why and then move into how and what. *Why*, in this sense, is defined as "your purpose, cause or belief" (Sinek, 2009, p. 39). The reason that why must come first is that "people don't buy WHAT you do, they buy WHY you do it" (p. 42). Sinek calls this the Golden Circle and suggests that our thinking, planning, and communicating move from the inside out (see below).

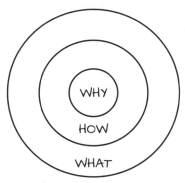

The Golden Circle
©Simon Sinek, Inc.

When we communicate what we are doing but leave out why we are doing it, it creates stress and doubt. Sinek's research even shows that it is harder for people to make decisions when they don't have the why behind it. Without a clear why, people search for endless data and quick fixes and then struggle to decide which path to take. But when there is a clear why, a communicated purpose, it leads to authenticity and trusting our gut instincts.

As teachers, the lesson here is that we must first get super clear on the why of our work, on our core beliefs, before we create plans for what and how we will teach.

As teachers, the lesson here is that we must first get super clear on the why of our work, on our core beliefs, before we create plans for what and how we will teach. In a sense, this book follows Sinek's Golden Circle in the way the chapters are organized. Here, in Chapter 2, we will focus on the why of our work—on our core beliefs as teachers. Then, once we have started with why, we will focus on what we do and how we do it in Chapters 3 through 6. If we are going to make the learning leaps of being our most effective and authentic teacher selves, we all benefit from starting with why.

Get Clear on Your Why

While working as a literacy coach in a suburban high school, I collaborated with Fiona, a tenth-grade English teacher, who wanted to try something new to engage and motivate her students. She explained that her third period class in particular consisted of self-proclaimed "nonreaders" who would do just about anything to avoid reading. Many of the students had individualized education plans, and reading was an area they struggled with. When I sat with Fiona, she explained how much she wanted her students to become readers, to develop self-confidence, and to have that experience of falling in love with a book and getting lost in its pages. As I listened to Fiona talk, I jotted down her why. I showed her the list, and we narrowed it down to two core beliefs she had about teaching readers. This was a mirroring conversation that I will discuss in detail later in the chapter. First, she wanted her students to experience the joy of reading. Second, she wanted them to have positive experiences with reading that would lead to self-confidence. She believed that joy and self-confidence were key elements in learning.

Align Your Why With Your What

Once we had these two core beliefs clearly articulated, we began to think about what we would do to create a classroom where students experienced joy and self-confidence-building experiences. This was a lot harder than we thought. If we knew what to do right away, we would have been doing it. So instead, we listed what she currently did. Then we reflected on each current practice to decide whether we would keep doing it based on two criteria: (1) Did it create joyful reading experiences? (2) Did it create positive and self-confidence-building experiences? If we could not answer yes to both questions, we crossed it off the list.

Well, this was a bit of a downer experience, as we realized that almost all of the current practices did not meet the criteria. For example, on the list she wrote "teach mostly classic literature" and "give weekly quizzes on each chapter" and "assign essays after each novel is finished." While each of these practices was common, they did not meet our criteria for joy and self-confidence. So I did some research and we met often—at least twice a week—to discuss other options.

The short version of our inquiry is that we decided to look at what brings us joy as readers and what kinds of experiences in the world (not just in English class) created self-confidence. We became annoying dinner party guests and family members as we interviewed our friends about their experiences with joy and self-confidence. We realized that much of what we found was also what authors such as Nancie Atwell (1989) in *In the Middle* and Kelly Gallagher (2009) in *Readicide* were writing about.

Decide on How

We decided to focus on more choices for students to decide what they were interested in reading and that we would explore a whole range of texts, not just classics, such as graphic novels, picture books, and young-adult novels, as well as articles and current events to build students' confidence with reading. This led to getting a grant to purchase books for the classroom library and to becoming book buddies with second graders. The classroom library gave students access to books they would actually enjoy reading, and the book buddies allowed students to read lower-level books to these younger students while building up their own fluency, comprehension, and most importantly, self-confidence.

As we co-planned lessons, we had some anchors to keep coming back to—joy and self-confidence. Of course, this didn't mean we could ignore standards and requirements, but it did mean we put our attention, focus, and energy into our core beliefs about what our students needed. When in doubt about a lesson, we would ask ourselves, "How is this helping the students develop joy and self-confidence for reading?" It became our mantra, so to speak.

Start With Why
★ Know your why.
★ Get clear on your what.
★ Decide on how.

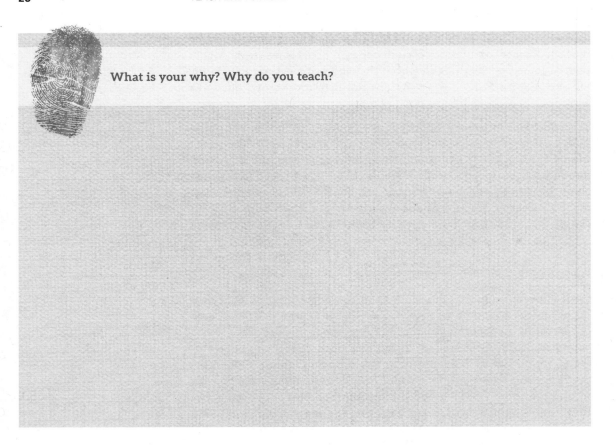

What is your why? Why do you teach?

Help Students Learn Like Themselves

We also built in time each week for student feedback and reflection so we could hear directly from students about how our new methods were going. While there are too many stories to share about just this class (in fact, it turned into a 300-plus-page dissertation for me), I will share just one.

Soraya was a student who told us early in the year that she "can't read." She spent many years in self-contained special education classes and took on the identify of a nonreader. Things started to change when she began reading higher-interest and lower-level books of her choosing under the guise of being a good book buddy to her second-grade partner. After a few months of focusing on joy and self-confidence, Soraya's science teacher came to talk to Fiona and me. The science teacher was upset because he kept catching Soraya reading her book under her desk when she was supposed to be listening to his science lecture and taking notes.

While we apologized for her being so disengaged from his class, we were also excited that she was choosing to read on her own time. When we asked her about it, she simply said what any avid reader would say: "It was such a good book that I couldn't put it down. I just had to know how it ended."

Every student in the third period class was interviewed, and every student explained that they did read more that year than the many years prior. They also acknowledged that the hard work they put into reading was paying off because they could see how much they had grown as readers. While not every student experienced utter joy and a deep sense of self-confidence, most of the students could be seen really reading, not just fake reading, on a regular basis and could explain what they were proud of about their growth that year. By focusing first on the why and then on the what and how, Fiona's students bought what she was selling—a love of reading—not because she told them what to do but because she helped them see why it was important.

CREATE STUDENT MOVEMENT

In his book *To Sell Is Human*, Daniel H. Pink (2012) explains that teachers are in the sales business. He does not define sales as simply trying to get someone to buy a product with money. He interviewed popular blogger and educator Larry Ferlazzo (2012), who described it "as teachers we want to move people" (p. 39). What he means by "move" is clarified:

> To sell well is to convince someone else to part with resources—not to deprive that person, but to leave him better off in the end. That is also what, say, a good algebra teacher does. At the beginning of a term, students don't know much about the subject. But the teacher works to convince his class to part with resources—time, attention, effort—and if they do, they will be better off when the term ends than they were when it began. (Ferlazzo, 2012, p. 39)

While most of us don't consider ourselves salespeople, thinking about our job as helping to move people does sort of sum up what we do. But Pink urges us not to think in outdated and stereotypical ways about sales. This is not a sleazy game of who can bluff the best as seen on TV portrayals of car salesmen.

Ferlazzo (2012) helps us distinguish between two ways to sell—to move people. The first he calls using irritation: "challenging people to do something that *we* want them to do" (p. 40). The second he calls using agitation: "challenging them to do something *they* want to do" (p. 40). Ferlazzo goes on to explain that using irritation may work in the short term, but to move students fully and over time, agitation works a whole lot better. He recommends we not look at students as a "pawn on the chessboard but as a full participant in the game" (p. 40).

So how does this connect with core beliefs and starting with why? Well, if we spend time considering our own core beliefs about teaching and learning, it helps us to also spend time getting to know our students' core beliefs—their why. In order to use agitation and get our students moving in productive ways, we need to know them well. Ferlazzo (2012) explains: "It means trying to elicit from people what their goals are for themselves and having the flexibility to frame what we do in that context" (p. 40). When we know what our students value and believe, we can shape the ways we teach and the choices we offer students to match. This is using agitation.

> When we know what our students value and believe, we can shape the ways we teach and the choices we offer students to match.

Here is an example from my third year of teaching third grade. For the previous few years, I taught students how to research by assigning them topics and then taking them step by step through the process. It took about eight weeks and was an excruciating process for both me and my students. By year three of this, I realized I needed to make a shift. Instead of assigning topics and going through my typical lessons, I began using agitation (I didn't call it agitation at the time, but now that I look back, I see that is what I was doing).

For the first two days of the research unit, I asked students to think about the topics they cared about and to list them in their research notebook. Then I asked them to pay attention to the world around them and to list observations and questions they had about it. I gave students time to meet with other students and discuss their lists and share ideas. By the end of those two days, students had filled pages with topics they wanted to explore. It was fascinating for me to see the topics they came up with. Two girls teamed up, and both had questions about hair. Yes, hair. They were so curious what it was made of and why we had it and how best to take care of it. Another pair of students was in love with our class pet, Spike, the guinea pig. They wanted to know much more about guinea pigs. Where did they come from? How did they become pets? How did they live in the wild? I mostly listened these first few days and got to know what *they* cared about and wanted.

By the third day, the students began class by asking me, "How do we find the answers to our questions?" They wanted to learn how to do research, which made the energy in the room bubble over with excitement. No one was forced to take notes, and no one asked how many pages their projects needed to be. This was because they were invested in real inquiry. I was able to shape my previously dull lessons about keyword searches, citations, and information verification into lessons that seemed to answer the questions they were asking me. For example, when students began to find conflicting information about a topic, I would say, "Maybe tomorrow we can learn how to verify that information is accurate." They believed they set the agenda, which in some ways they did. While I was going to teach that lesson anyway, when I decided to teach it was flexible to match the students.

By the end of the month (yes, it took only one month instead of two months like the previous years), every student had finished the research with a teaching visual and a written product. There was so much movement that month, and it all began when I found out what my students valued and used agitation, challenging them to do what *they* wanted. I realized that what people value is what moves them through the world.

I didn't just use agitation with the whole class but also one on one with students. For example, in that same class I had a student, Patrick, who refused to write about his reading. He never used his reading notebook and would rather "just read" than ever jot down any thinking about his reading. I would sit side by side with him and ask him what he was learning from his books and he could clearly and vividly explain it to me, but when it came time to writing it down he would just stare at the page. It got to the point where I was worried he would not be able to pass the grade-level state exam, which while not the most important aspect of our class did have an impact on his ability to pass the third grade in this state. I knew that irritation was not working for him; I could not get him to do it because I wanted him to. Instead, I needed to use agitation, figuring out what *he* wanted and using that to help him engage more with writing about this reading.

I asked him, "What are you learning about in your books?" and "Who else do you think would want to learn what you are learning?" and "How could you become a teacher of this topic to others?" Through this questioning, I found out that Patrick loved reading about birds; wanted to do some bird-watching; and that he recently discovered field guides, which is what he now loved to study. By the end of the conversation, he realized that he could make his own field guide to native birds to our local area. He made a plan for what he would record and how he would do it. While it was not a full jump into the formal writing about reading that would be tested, he was now seeing the value of jotting down what he learned so he could incorporate it into his own field guide. This was an important first step to having Patrick realize the power of writing about reading, based on what he valued and wanted to learn. Whenever I encounter a student who just won't do something that I value, I tend to shift gears to figure out what the student values and begin there.

> What people value is what moves them through the world.

In what ways do you already "sell" your students on your class? How else might you use agitation to garner even more student engagement?

THREE WAYS TO KNOW AND NAME YOUR CORE BELIEFS

It takes purposeful time and self-reflection to uncover our most core beliefs—our why. No one else can tell you what lies inside of your Golden Circle, but I can offer three ways that have helped me and many other teachers in their uncovering process. The following three practices may help you.

- Describe what success looks like in your classroom.

- Keep a question journal about your curiosities.

- Have mirroring conversations with trusted colleagues to gain perspective.

Describe What Success Looks Like

Think about this question: What does success look like for my students? On the face of it, this question looks like a what question, and I just spent a few pages telling you that we benefit from starting with why. But if we dig deeper, we can see that this is really a why question disguised with the word *what*. This is because it helps to visualize and to feel what success would be like to better understand what we believe. What we believe is our why—it is our purpose and our core. Confusing? Let's just get to practicing it and see what I mean.

Use Your Imagination

Picture yourself in your classroom. It doesn't need to be your current classroom at all. Make it your ideal classroom. What does it look like? Feel like? Sound like? Allow yourself to be in make-believe land, and really go for what your idea of success would be. Go back to your childlike self when you would daydream about your life. Let yourself daydream about your picture of perfect when it comes to teaching and learning. If you are a visual thinker, then try sketching what you pictured. If you are more of a wordsmith, then jot down descriptions of what you saw and felt. Record your ideals and daydreams.

Use your imagination.

List Precise Words

Now go back and look at your sketch or description. Pay attention to each part, and list precise words for each one. For example, my list today includes the following:

- Taking intellectual risks
- Listening with curiosity to others
- Embracing the challenges
- Creating space for everyone's ideas

Notice how my list has very specific verbs (taking, listening, embracing, creating). It also is succinct. If I can't say it in a short phrase or line, it likely has too many parts to it. For example, if I start with this longer line—Create classroom experiences where everyone can be themselves and learn in their own ways and want to come to class each day—I may break it into a few different and succinct parts:

- Include everyone
- Encourage learning in different ways
- Create joyful learning in class

Once you have your list, test it out. Does it ring true for you? Does it feel right? Which words and phrases do you feel the most charge about? Bold those words, and then carry them with you for a few days or weeks. I don't mean you literally have to carry them with you, but it may help. Post them around your classroom, or write them in bright fancy letters on your planner or screensaver. How do they feel day after day? Do they leave you with more energy? Ready to go be your best teaching self? If not, go back and imagine again. Allow yourself to dream bigger.

Make Your Box Bigger

One of my mentors, Seth Godin, designed a workshop called the altMBA, where students from all professions and all around the world come together to find their core beliefs, and then learn how to put them in action—what Seth calls to "ship" them. A key assignment in the workshop involves each student realizing how big or small they create the box of possibility around themselves. This helps us realize just how small we tend to think when we dream up what we think is possible. He asks us to make the box of possibility even bigger. What could we do if we didn't believe it was not possible? What I learned from the assignment when I was a student was how difficult it was for me to make the box bigger. I kept being my own naysayer and telling myself I couldn't do it. From this, I realized I could benefit from a lot more purposeful dreaming. By simply asking "What if?," I was able to remove some barriers that I was creating to possibility and uncover what I really believed.

Try it yourself. Look at your list of what success looks like. Ask yourself, "Can it be bigger?" Or consider, "Am I being a naysayer to my own vision?" If so, give yourself some credit. You don't need to live every ideal on your second day of teaching. It will take time to align your core beliefs with your practice, but knowing what your real, true, big beliefs are helps you take the first step in creating the reality.

> It will take time to align your core beliefs with your practice, but knowing what your real, true, big beliefs are helps you take the first step in creating the reality.

Describe What Success Looks Like

★ Use your imagination.

★ List precise words.

★ Make your box bigger.

What is your vision of success for students? Be precise with your description and words, and then consider how you can make the box bigger.

Keep a Question Journal

A second practice for knowing and naming your core beliefs is to keep a journal of all the questions you find yourself asking about teaching and learning. Then, notice the kinds of questions you tend to ask. My husband, John, recommended this practice to me, and at first I rolled my eyes. Sorry, John. I just didn't see how questions could get at core beliefs. It wasn't until I tried it myself that I understood its power. Here are the steps I took to create and then really reflect on my questions.

Pay Attention to Questions

This may sound so obvious, but when I first began my question journal, I was stuck and had nothing to write down. I literally stared at a blank page. I was not used to paying attention to the questions I was asking myself all day. By simply deciding to keep the question journal, it brought my questions to the forefront. I noticed the questions I was asking about my teaching, my students, and about learning. I kept my journal handy so I could quickly jot down the question and then go back to what I was doing. Other days I didn't have time to write them until the end of the day, and that worked too, as a sort of reflection on the day.

Here are a few things I learned from paying attention to my questions. I asked myself a lot more questions than I realized. I also tended to ask a lot of *how* questions, such as "How do I know if my students are really understanding what I am teaching?" and "How can I encourage more student conversation and engagement?" and "How do I get to know each student in the small amount of time I have with them?" I noticed that lots of questions were about the parts of my day that I thought could have gone better. For example, I asked questions about assessment, collaboration, and timing of the lessons. In addition, I seemed to ask questions about the parts of my teaching that I felt the most insecure about. And, interestingly, I tended to ask questions about the parts I felt most confident about, such as "Why did today's writing workshop go so well?" and "Why are my writing lessons so engaging to students?" By paying attention and jotting down my questions, I was able to get to know myself as a teacher even better.

Don't Answer the Questions

This may sound odd, but it is important to not answer the questions in your journal. It is not a question *and* answer journal. This is because one of my teacher mentors taught me that as soon as we think we have an answer, we stop being curious. This nonanswering stance allows us to be open and to ask the questions again and again. At first it may feel uncomfortable to ask the question and not try to figure it out, but by rereading the questions you jotted down on a regular basis, without the answers, it allows you to revisit them and go even deeper. Some of my most powerful questions came from rereading previous lists of questions. One example follows.

Original Question: How Do I Get my Students to Write More?

Additional questions generated by the original:

★ Why do some students write more than others?

★ How does choice of writing topic affect the amount of writing?

★ How can I offer students more time to write in class?

★ What strategies seemed to generate the most amount of writing?

★ Is more writing the goal?

★ What would happen if I focused on quality instead of quantity of writing?

Categorize Your Questions

Once you have lots of questions, begin to read and categorize them by theme. This process is not about putting labels on your questions or on yourself and instead is about finding patterns so you can get to know your core beliefs. For example, if you notice you have a lot of questions about student motivation, it may mean you really believe that motivation is key. Or if you have a lot of questions about balancing individual and group work, it may mean you believe that helping students work well on their own and with a group is essential. Find the patterns, and then turn them into statements of belief. Here are a couple of mine based on the writing question examples I just shared.

★ I believe that students benefit from lots of time to practice a skill.

★ I believe that students need to feel invested in a topic to write about it.

Give a question journal a try, and see what you uncover about your core beliefs. If you already keep a journal, set aside some pages or a section for questions. If you don't regularly journal, then have fun picking one out that speaks to you. Or if you are a digital writer, start a Google Doc file so you can access it on any device, or use your phone's notes app to

> As soon as we think we have an answer, we stop being curious.

keep a running list. No matter the format, embrace your own curiosities by paying attention to your questions about teaching and learning, and then use them to name your core beliefs.

Keep a Question Journal

★ Pay attention to questions.

★ Don't answer the questions.

★ Categorize your questions.

Get started on your question journal right now. List a few of the questions you are thinking about.

Have Mirroring Conversations

So far, I shared two ways to name your core beliefs—describing what success looks like to you and keeping a question journal. A third way to uncover your beliefs is to enlist a friend, coach, or mentor for mirroring conversations. A mirroring conversation is one where you don't give advice or try to fix anything for each other, and instead, you simply listen and clarify and then mirror back what you just heard. Most of us can't really see or hear ourselves accurately. This is because our filter through which we view ourselves is distorted with our identity, our histories, and our stories. A friend can listen and help us hear what we are really trying to say with much more clarity than we can figure out on our own. Another benefit of having mirroring conversations is that you make time to reflect and do the work of uncovering your core beliefs. It can be so challenging to set aside time for personal reflection and having a partner gives us accountability as well as support.

Set Up a Framework

When beginning mirroring conversations for the first time, it is helpful to set up a framework so both people know what to expect and what their role is. What follows is an example of a framework I like to use.

1. Decide ahead of time how long you have to spend on the conversation. Then discuss if you will both have time to be the speaker and mirror or if today's conversation will be each of you in the one role.

2. The speaker thinks about which belief she wants to talk about.

3. The speaker shares her thinking about this belief with as much detail as she thinks is needed. The speaker also pauses for the mirror to reflect back what he is hearing in between main ideas.

4. The mirror says back what he heard without any opinions, judgments, or interpretations. He may say something like "I heard you say... " and then "Is that what you meant?"

5. The speaker either acknowledges that is what she said or clarifies it based on what is needed.

6. After the given time or when the conversation seems finished, both people take a few quiet minutes to list the core beliefs they heard. The mirror hands the list to the speaker so that she has both her copy and his copy to compare and refer back to.

While this may sound super formal, in reality it goes quite smoothly once the framework is established. If you don't want to use this exact outline, that is fine. I do, however, suggest you stick to number four on this list, no matter the format. This is because it is easy for the conversation to turn into a session on helping the speaker come up with her core beliefs and implanting our own beliefs as the speaker's. Rather than do this, it is super helpful to simply listen and repeat what you heard. As the mirror, you may not feel like you are doing much, but it is so supportive to serve as a listener who can reflect back to us what we are really saying.

Listen for Your Own Truth

When it is your time to listen and mirror, it may help you clarify what you believe by hearing someone else's thinking. I can't tell you how many times I have heard someone say something and thought, "Yes, that is exactly what I was trying to say." While we don't want to just copy our friends and colleagues because it is easier than doing the digging ourselves, it can be just the thing to hear another person's language and phrasing around a belief we knew we carried and just didn't know how to articulate.

Sometimes when we hear someone else's core beliefs, it hits us in our own core. We have likely all had experiences when someone says something and we feel like they have been eavesdropping in our brains. By choosing a mirroring partner who you know to have similar beliefs as you, it may help you uncover more of your own. It is not cheating to write down some of the beliefs you heard and state them as your own—as long as you know you believe them too.

Listen for the Other Person's Truth

Other times it may be helpful to ask a colleague you know who has very different beliefs than you do to be a mirroring partner. While it may feel awkward and even painful to sit through someone else's sharing about beliefs you oppose, there is also a lot to be gained from learning to simply listen and mirror. In her book *Braving the Wilderness*, best-selling author and social worker Brené Brown (2017) explains that we do not have to agree with one another to feel connection. By simply bearing witness to one another, we can feel that connection and help one another show up bravely as ourselves. As I write those words, I know I have a lot to learn about how to do this. I tend to interrupt when I hear something that goes against my core beliefs or judge them in my head. But I can't be fully present and listen if I am doing this. It is quite a powerful practice—one that I am working on daily—to simply listen and mirror so both myself and the speaker can truly hear what is being said. Even if at the end of the conversation I still believe I have nothing in common with this person, it will at least help me get clearer on what I do not believe. And I can learn to do this in a professional and humane way.

Have Mirroring Conversations

★ Set up a framework.

★ Listen for your own truth.

★ Listen for the other person's truth.

Who do you want to have a mirroring conversation with? How will you approach them to get started?

> ## Ways To Uncover Your Core Beliefs
>
> ★ **Describe What Success Looks Like**
>
> - Use your imagination.
> - List precise words.
> - Make your box bigger.
>
> ★ **Keep a Question Journal**
>
> - Pay attention to your questions.
> - Don't answer your questions.
> - Categorize your questions.
>
> ★ **Mirror Conversations**
>
> - Set up a framework.
> - Listen for your own truth.
> - Listen for another person's truth.

UNCOVER YOUR STUDENTS' BELIEFS

Now that we discussed ways to uncover our own core beliefs, let's turn to learning more about what our students hold dear. As I explained earlier in the chapter, we can start with why and use agitation to move students, but this requires us to know our students' why and what they want and believe. When we know our students well, we can design lessons and experiences that tap into their natural curiosity and excitement for learning. Luckily, the same practices we can use to uncover our own core beliefs also work with students. Let's notice the parallel between our own search for meaning and our students' desires.

Students' Descriptions of Success

Just like we can spend time daydreaming about our ideal and our visions of what a successful classroom experience would be like, our students can do the same. We can explicitly ask them what success looks like to them. If your students are too young to really understand the word *success*, you can substitute it with a word they do understand. For younger students, you may ask them to draw a picture of their ideal learning environment. For older students, you may ask them to interview a partner about their view of success and then introduce that partner with the descriptions they heard. Or you can ask students to share a story of a time they felt really successful and why they thought so. Find any way that will allow students to honestly share what they believe about success and then take note so you can use this to help move your students toward what they want.

Student Question Journals

Students can tab off a section in a class journal or create a shared Google Doc and keep track of the questions they have. Just like we teachers can pay attention to our questions, jot them down, and categorize them, students can do the same. These questions can be about learning in general or about the topic you teach in particular. By knowing their questions, it can help you frame your teaching around what they are genuinely curious about.

Student-Led Conversations

While most teachers say there is limited time to sit side by side with students during the school day, it is always worthwhile. By giving each student a few minutes of your undivided attention, you can be a mirror to them. Ask them to share their beliefs about learning or how they are doing and then, rather than judge or share your opinions, simply mirror back what you heard. If you want to learn more about how to serve as mirrors to students, you may want to check out a previous book I wrote called *Mindsets and Moves* (Goldberg, 2015). You can also teach students the framework for how to be mirrors to one another. This allows you to move around the classroom and listen to what they say, which often is a bit more honest when talking to a peer rather than the teacher.

Uncover Your Students' Beliefs

★ Students can share their descriptions of success.

★ Students can keep track of their questions.

★ Students can lead reflection conversations.

Ask your students to do one of the previously given exercises, and then jot down any trends you see emerging from their beliefs. How can you incorporate the student beliefs into your classroom design?

COME BACK TO WHY

Exploring and uncovering our own core vision of teaching is not something that happens only at the beginning of our teaching career or beginning of a new school year. It is so important that we revisit our why on a regular and ongoing basis.

In this chapter, we learned about starting with why because our core beliefs are what will guide our every teaching practice. When we start with why, we get to know ourselves and our students better and can be that authentic and effective teacher we most want to be. Exploring and uncovering our own core vision of teaching is not something that happens only at the beginning of our teaching career or beginning of a new school year.

It is so important that we revisit our why on a regular and ongoing basis. This is especially helpful on bad days, tough months, and even during the years we think we will not last all school year. And this is true when we are in the teaching zone and everything is working so darn well. When we are clear on our inner circle and we are able to name our core beliefs as they stand today, right now, we can make choices that are in alignment with teaching like our true selves. In the next chapter, I will help us match our teaching to our core beliefs so that our values are not just platitudes on our wall but actionable daily practices. In Chapter 5, we will revisit our questions and use them to drive our professional growth.

Reread everything you wrote from Chapters 1 and 2 so far, then write down your current response to this question: What are your core beliefs about teaching and learning?

VIEW
TEACHING AS A PRACTICE

Video 3

Source: One 21 Production

"It doesn't happen all at once," said the Skin Horse. "You become. It takes a long time. That's why it doesn't happen often to people who break easily, or have sharp edges, or who have to be carefully kept. Generally, by the time you are Real, most of your hair has been loved off, and your eyes drop out and you get loose in the joints and very shabby. But these things don't matter at all, because once you are Real you can't be ugly, except to people who don't understand."

—Margery Williams Bianco, *The Velveteen Rabbit*

After several years of practicing yoga, I decided to take a yoga teacher training program. I loved yoga; it calmed me, made me feel good, and I wanted to know more about how it actually works. I also wanted to be able to lead my own classes. A few weeks into the program, many of us prospective yoga teachers felt super self-conscious about our teaching. When we led our classmates in short practice yoga classes, we would stumble over our words, get stuck and freeze, or break out in a massive sweat (which is not so attractive when you are already wearing spandex).

To help us out, Julie, one of the teacher trainers, called us in a circle and turned off the lights. She had us sit down and close our eyes. She explained that she was going to have us move our bodies into a pose we loved, and she wanted us to narrate what we were doing as we did it. No one said anything, so Julie went first. Our eyes were closed, so we could not see what she was doing, but we could hear what she was narrating, and she asked us to join her: "I am flexing my feet. I am stretching my arms up tall. I am taking a deep breath in." We followed her words with our own movements. When it was my turn, I found an easy calm to it, nothing like I had ever experienced in my previous teaching. I narrated each move and felt like myself.

After we each had a turn, the lights were turned back on, we opened our eyes, and we reflected with each other about the experience. We all had almost the same response. By focusing on our own body movements and using our own language to talk about what we were doing, it felt natural, comfortable, and instinctual. We were not trying to play the role of yoga teacher or guess the right way to call the moves of a pose. We simply listened to the wisdom of our bodies and followed its lead. Julie helped us see that prior to this experience we were overthinking our teaching and disconnecting from all our experience and knowledge. We had been so focused on getting it right that we lost touch with ourselves.

> When I practice teaching, I also try things out, take chances, reflect, and learn from each moment what is working or not working for my students.

When I walked home from yoga teacher training that night, I kept thinking about my classroom teaching and how Julie's message about teaching yoga was so helpful for me in all aspects of my teaching life. Yoga is called a practice. We don't say, "I do yoga." We say, "I practice yoga." This nuance in language choice is a vital element of yoga. Yogi Trish Huston (2013) says that to practice means "to try things that we can't already do—to take chances, to make mistakes, and in short, to learn." We practice yoga to quiet our minds, to become more flexible, and to be more present in the moments. But what does it mean to practice teaching? When I practice teaching, I also try things out, take chances, reflect, and learn from each moment what is working or not working for my students. What do you think of when you think of the word *practice*?

FOUR TYPES OF PRACTICE

As a young soccer player, I had multiple coaches tell me, "Practice doesn't make perfect. It makes permanent." My teen self would roll my eyes at this advice, but now I see there is something to it. When we practice the same way over and over again, we are training our brains and bodies to do it that same way in the future (regardless of whether it works). Not all practice is the same. Let's think about the types of practice we all do and how we can consciously choose what we do and how we hone our teaching practice. As teachers, we can create routines through repetitive practice, create solutions through original practice, create awareness through mindful practice, and create instincts through playful practice. All types of practice are necessary when we enter our classrooms each day.

Create Routines: Repetitive Practice

Think about the way you brush your teeth. You likely have one way you do this day after day and night after night. You don't even think about the way you brush anymore. This sort of repetitive practice is helpful for learning a new skill. When you were a toddler, that repeated practice was really important for your now-adult oral hygiene. Best-selling author Seth Godin explains more about repetitive practice. It is when you "move asymptotically toward perfection. Practice your technique and your process to get yourself ever more skilled at doing it to spec. This is the practice of grand slalom, of arithmetic, of learning your lines" (Godin, 2017b).

Repetitive practice is appropriate when we are learning something that can be done with very similar or exact techniques time after time and without many unknown factors or contexts. An example of repetitive practice for a learner might be when a first grader is practicing letter formation. But, of course, there are also many aspects of teaching and learning that do have moving parts, multiple factors, and varying contexts, and for these parts of our work, we benefit from other types of practice.

Create Solutions: Original Practice

Another type of practice is viewing each experience as an opportunity to make a purposeful, conscious choice and then reflect on how it went. This sort of practice is about creating something that you hope will work but know may not work right away for every student or each class. Seth Godin (2017b) explains, "This is the practice of failure. Of creating original work that doesn't succeed until it does. Of writing, oration and higher-level math in search of an elusive outcome, even a truth, one that might not even be there. We become original through practice." Since our students are not all the same and how they learn is never all the same, we can't assume all of our tried-and-true lessons will always work. In fact, they rarely do.

When we view our teacher role as meeting our unique students' learning needs, then we see the value of original practice. Original practice allows us to create something new for our students that is meant for them and their learning right now. When you realize a student is confused about a concept you have been teaching for a week or more, you rely on creating an original practice to try something new that may just work this time.

While leading a workshop with high school social studies teachers who were concerned about their students' abilities to read complex, primary sources, I began by listening to the teachers' observations about their students. What at first sounded like a venting session really was a reflective conversation about everything the teachers noticed that their students needed to learn. They shared stories of students who stopped reading after the first few lines and struggled with stamina. They also recalled how most of their students skipped over unfamiliar vocabulary without even trying to figure it out. They acknowledged the long sentences and archaic language choices that many of their historical sources used. As I listened and listed the challenges, I realized just how complicated the teaching of historical documents really is. There were not established routines that could just be rolled out and used to create a solution.

Since each student was different, each document was different, and each teacher was different, we needed to create some original practices that could be tried out and then reflected on and refined as needed. We ended up breaking into small groups of teachers, each group choosing a primary source they wanted to teach, and then reading it line by line, reflecting on what strategies they were each using to make sense of the text. We shared our strategies and realized which ones were similar and which ones were different from one another's. Then we used the list we created to make charts we could use to teach students based on what they would benefit from learning next. The teachers left the workshop feeling prepared to offer different strategies to their unique students, based on what they observed each one needed. While we did not have foolproof routines, we had ideas to try, and then we planned on meeting again in a few weeks to reflect and revise our plans together. What stands out to me here is that the teachers had the space to reflect on their own routines and how to make sense of them, and they learned additional techniques from their colleagues.

Create Awareness: Mindful Practice

One of my yoga teacher mentors often says, "Never arrive in the pose." What she means is that when we think we have arrived and landed in perfection we become stuck and stop paying attention to the small nuances. We become mindless and miss the opportunity to bend a bit deeper or breathe a bit fuller. The same can be said of our teaching practice. We don't want to think we have arrived because then we miss the opportunities to learn even more.

What my yoga teacher is referring to is what Harvard professor Ellen Langer studies and what she calls maintaining a mindful state. Langer (2016) spent decades studying learning and found that much of what we learn and practice is actually what she calls "overlearned skills," where we drill ourselves in a certain skill so it becomes second nature (p. 13). She claims that when we overlearn a skill, "mindless practice keeps the activity from becoming our own" (Langer, 2016, p. 14). This overlearning leads to teaching that fails to acknowledge the contexts and conditions that make something true.

On the other hand, "teaching skills and facts in a conditional way sets the stage for doubt and an awareness of how different situations may call for subtle differences in what we bring to them" (Langer, 2016, p. 15). In this case, doubt is a good thing because it keeps the learners engaged in continuous mindful thinking. Going back to my yoga example, if my instructor does not teach in conditional ways then I would likely injure myself. One possible condition could be tight hamstrings. If I don't adjust the pose for my tightness, I could pull or strain a muscle. Being aware of the conditions of learning allows us to practice mindfully.

Langer (2016) and her research team found that mindful practice entails certain psychological states including openness to novelty, sensitivity to different contexts, and orientation in the present (p. 23). I realized that while we cannot control who our students are and what they will enter our classrooms already knowing how to do, we do have control over our own framing of our practice as teachers. I began to ask myself how I could approach my curriculum and my students with an open stance. I also worked to make sure I was not ignoring the different contexts that the learning would be happening within. And like almost every other teacher I have met, being oriented to the present moments with my students continues to be a daily intention for me.

During my first year as a literacy coach, I found myself in a preK classroom of four-year-olds. I entered that room of very tiny humans and found myself second-guessing everything I knew about teaching, because I had almost no experience with children under age five. I was there to help the classroom teacher, Ingrid, support her students with beginning writing strategies. I began by sitting in a circle on the carpet with the students, and I told them a true story from my own life. Then I took out a blank piece of paper and modeled how I drew a picture to match my story. I showed students that writers use symbols and pictures to tell stories. After I finished modeling, students turned to a partner and told a true story about themselves. Then they went back to their tables and used their markers to draw their stories. As students worked on their drawings, the classroom teacher and I sat down with tables of students to get to know them as writers and to coach them with strategies as needed.

We did not have a script of exactly what each student was going to need us to say or do. Ingrid sat with one table and noticed that a boy drew scribbles all over his page. Rather than judge his work, she kept an open stance and asked him, "What are you drawing?" The boy looked up and said, "This is me and my three brothers." The teacher still was confused because she just saw scribbles, so she kept being open and asked another question: "Can you show me what you are doing in your picture?" The boy put his marker down and pointed to different parts of the page and explained, "My big brother is so big and loud. My little brother is so annoying, and my baby brother just cries all the time. I am over here playing with my Legos." As he told his story, he pointed to a different corner of the picture to match what he was saying. There was a different color for each brother and different-size scribbles for each one too. So what looked like random scribbles did represent a real story with real characters to this four-year-old student.

While the teacher had an idea in her mind of what an exemplary preK writer would do, namely draw people with a circle for a head and arms and legs and a face, she did not leave the present moment with her student. She noted what this student could do and then jotted down some notes for herself. Only then did she think about what she might model for him next time—how to sketch a person using shapes. Rather than shut down as a writer due to a teacher forcing him to redo his picture, the writer left that experience feeling proud. The next day Ingrid pulled out a few books that had simple pictures with shapes as people. She showed this to the student so he had some contexts to see how people look in books and how illustrators use drawings to tell stories. Even though the teacher had been teaching for over thirty years, she did not approach her students in only routine ways. Instead, she was using mindful practice to develop awareness of her students' strengths, strategies, and potential next steps.

Create Instincts: Playful Practice

In addition to repetitive, original, and mindful practice, playful practice helps us develop our teaching instincts. While play sounds like something that only very young children practice, bringing playfulness into your daily practice is essential for purposeful teaching. Boston College professor Peter Gray is an evolutionary developmental psychologist, which means he studies how as a human species we have evolved as learners and the repercussions of when free play is excluded or limited from people's lives. In his popular book *Free to Learn*, Gray (2013) explains our natural drives as human learners. One drive is that of curiosity, which propels us to be explorers of the world. Another drive is that of playfulness, which propels us to practice new skills and use them creatively. When people are curious and playful, they are free to learn in natural and instinctual ways. This does not mean we teachers need to buy Legos or dust off our Cabbage Patch Kids, but it does mean we bring a playful attitude toward our teaching.

Gray (2013) explains, "Play is serious, yet not serious; trivial yet profound; imaginative and spontaneous, yet bound by rules and anchored in the real world. It is childish, yet underlies many of the greatest accomplishments of adults" (p. 136). One of the major ways I have brought playfulness into my teaching is by being a co-learner in my classroom. Rather than focus on lessons and experiences where I already know the answers, I offer students experiences where there is not one clear answer, and I have the opportunity to explore and imagine with my students.

One example of playful practice is when I was serving as a professor, teaching seniors in the preservice education department. During a content area literacy class, I had several preservice math teachers who were feeling left out. I created a real-life problem that called upon all of the students to use both their content area knowledge and literacy skills. My good friend Renee had just moved to Los Angeles after living in New York City for over a decade. She needed to get a car and wanted help with this large purchase. She video conferenced into our classroom and explained her situation. Should she buy or lease? Should she get a new or used car? Which type of car? Why? After the video call, the students worked during the next week in small groups to come to their own conclusion. They researched loan and lease rates, figured out gas costs, created budgets, and argued pros and cons of the choices. The following week they presented their findings to Renee and their rationale for the recommendations. I approached this experience without having an answer in mind. I was a co-learner in this classroom too, and I brought a playful lens into my teaching practice. As a result, every student was engaged and so was I. As an added bonus, Renee made a sound decision about which car to get.

Types of Practice

★ Create routines through repetitive practice.

★ Create solutions through original practice.

★ Create awareness through mindful practice.

★ Create instincts through playful practice.

What types of practice do you tend to do? Which types might you want to do more of? How will you get started?

YOUR PERSONAL POWER

Researcher Amy Cuddy's (2015) book *Presence: Bringing Your Boldest Self to Your Biggest Challenges* explains what personal power is and how it affects our ability to practice our core beliefs. Unlike social power, which is power over other people, personal power is our ability to control our own states and behaviors. Holocaust survivor and author Elie Wiesel explains, "Ultimately, the only power to which man should aspire is that which he exercises over himself." As Cuddy's research shows, we cannot achieve something without feeling personally powerful. She quotes Joe Magee, a New York University professor, who claims, "Personal power is all about having confidence to act based on one's own beliefs, attitudes, and values, and having the sense that one's actions will be effective." While we can't always feel personally powerful and we will all have our self-confidence tested, Cuddy's research found that we can prime ourselves to feel more personally powerful.

> "Personal power is all about having confidence to act based on one's own beliefs, attitudes, and values, and having the sense that one's actions will be effective."
> —Joe Magee

Having supported and collaborated with thousands of teachers, one common theme shines through. When teachers lack a sense of personal power, they end up disconnecting and disengaging from their work and no one would blame them. When I think back to the times when I "dialed it in," they were all times when I felt powerless. For example, one year the math leaders in my district decided teachers could not be trusted to see the unit math tests before they were to be given. As a result, we were sent the tests the morning they were to be administered. My colleagues and I were both angry for feeling in the dark but also hurt that we were not given the respect and trust we felt we deserved. We were not going to teach directly to the test, but it seemed nonsensical to prepare students for a unit assessment when we didn't even know the expectations for the end. Our math scores were rather low that year; we sat with arms crossed at math team meetings; and only finally, when the leadership team asked for feedback, did we explain just how apathetic and powerless we felt. Luckily our leaders listened and changed this policy the following year, and when our sense of personal power came back so did our math scores and our energy for teaching.

Sometimes in our teaching careers, when we feel powerless we unfortunately go radio silent when we could be speaking up so others can hear us and help us. We have to be the ones to empower ourselves. I had the privilege of supporting a team of fourth-grade teachers who were given a new writing approach and curriculum to try out. They had little background knowledge and expertise in how to teach writing in this new way. Instead of succumbing to a powerless feeling, they took action. First, they used their common planning time to plan and write together. Once they mapped out the unit a bit more, they looked at student writing samples to reflect on all they had been successful in teaching their students so far. From this place of confidence, they decided to team up and co-teach some of their planned lessons. They brought classes together into one room and took turns teaching the whole class lesson before the students went off to write on their own. By co-planning, acknowledging past success, and co-teaching, they helped prime each other for a greater sense of personal power, and they also had a lot of fun teaching writing that year.

Prime Yourself for Feeling Powerful

Since feeling powerful has a huge impact on our lives, it would be amazing if we could create this feeling on demand. Cuddy's (2015) research found that we can trigger ourselves to feel more powerful, which leads to a whole array of positive outcomes. She explains that power can be turned on like a switch that affects our thoughts, feelings, and behaviors. All we have to do in order to turn on the switch is to think back on a time in our lives when we felt personally powerful. We can recall the feelings, the self-confidence, and the actions that went along with the powerful memory. This is called being primed. When we are primed, we flip the switch, and the simple thought exercise shifts us into feeling powerful rather than powerless. What I love about priming ourselves to feel powerful is that it is free: We can do it anytime and anywhere. We can use little nudges to conjure our boldest and most true selves.

The next time you walk into your classroom, you can take one minute to prime yourself for power. If it seems too easy to be true, then think about the opposite and how when we think of powerless experiences we end up feeling deflated. Her research is fascinating on many levels, but for me the most helpful part is that while the science is complicated the practice is not. We can choose to feel more powerful by choosing how we prime ourselves as teachers.

My friend Angie Fifer is a performance psychologist who works with professional and NCAA athletes as well as military personnel. She uses priming all of the time with her clients. She once shared a technique at a workshop at which we co-presented that has become a regular practice in my own teaching life. She explained how college basketball players who take free throws are constantly being threatened by distractions and opponents trying to "get in their heads." The opposing team's fans sit behind the basket and wave their hands back and forth as they yell, scream, and bang their feet on the bleachers. The noise is deafening, and if they don't focus, the players will almost always get psyched out and miss the free throw. So Angie helps the players prime themselves for success and a feeling of personal power. First, during practice, she has them approach the free throw line in exactly the same way every time to

> Sometimes in our teaching careers, when we feel powerless we unfortunately go radio silent when we could be speaking up so others can hear us and help us. We have to be the ones to empower ourselves.

build a consistent routine. Second, she has them look at the ball as they bounce or grab it and then at the net as they shoot. She has them block out everything else. Third, right before they shoot they say a positive word or phrase to themselves that they use every single time they shoot a free throw to remind them of their past success. This priming routine has proven very successful for her players. When they feel personally powerful, they make more of their baskets, which contributes to more long-term confidence.

We can borrow and revise Angie's priming strategy and use it in our classrooms. We can use planning time to practice a strategy or method during the non–game time. Then we can create a routine that has led to success in the past. Finally, we can create our own mantra of words and phrases that remind us of our past success. For example, I often tell myself when I am running up a steep hill in a triathlon, "Your body is a machine. You got this." And when I am about to speak in public I often tell myself, "You are so lucky to be here. Speak your truth."

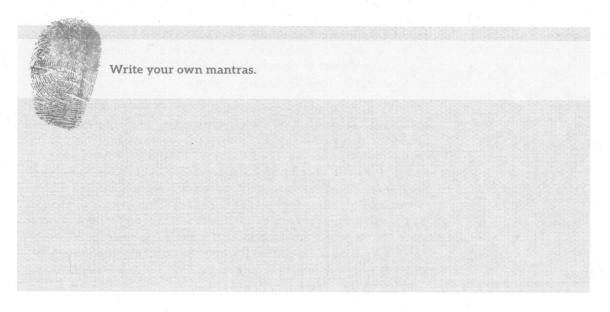

Write your own mantras.

Don't Make Every Day Game Day

What if every day was the big test, the race, or the championship game? When we make each day the big event, it turns it into a high-stakes experience. While many of us can rise to the occasion during a race or test, no one I know wants each day to be filled with that sort of pressure. Instead, we want to feel like our classrooms are safe spaces to take risks. Cuddy (2015) explains how our own sense of power influences how we

> When we haven't primed ourselves for power and instead approach our classrooms from a place of powerlessness, we create anxiety for ourselves.

rise or fall when we face a pressurized experience. When we haven't primed ourselves for power and instead approach our classrooms from a place of powerlessness, we create anxiety for ourselves. When we feel powerless, "lucidity abandons us, and our brains become unable to meet the demands of complicated or stressful situations ... the anxiety that results from it undermines executive function.... With impaired executive functioning, we become less effective at updating mental information, inhibiting unwanted impulses, and planning future actions" (Cuddy, 2015, p. 119). As a teacher, I never want to be without my executive functioning abilities, because teaching is a profession, more than most, that requires us to use that part of our brains.

The lesson here for us teachers is to prime ourselves for a sense of personal power when we enter into the oftentimes pressurized world of our classrooms but also not to add more pressure to our days. Not surprisingly, people who feel personal power have self-confidence that helps them interpret competitive experiences as improving their performance. They rise to the occasion. When people approach the same sort of experiences from a place of powerlessness, they report having less self-confidence and that the competitive anxiety they experienced inhibited their performance. A review of 114 studies found that "when people possess a strong belief that they will be able to perform the task at hand, they are more likely to perform it" (Cuddy, 2015, p. 133).

The practice I use most for relieving pressure is a perspective exercise. I ask myself, "Does this lesson or experience need to be so high stakes?" The answer is almost always no! Instead of approaching each day as the championship game, I give myself permission to view each day and each lesson as practice for game day. I ask myself questions like "What did I teach today?" and "What did I learn today?" every single day. Then I think about what I want to do differently next time and what I want to store away to do again. In every single lesson I ever taught, there is something that went well and something that I could have done differently. This is what it means to practice teaching. By expecting success and challenges in each lesson, I am setting up the day to be less pressurized and less high stakes.

It's Not All About Me

One more fascinating finding from Cuddy's research on power has to do with its correlation to self-focus and anxiety. She found that when we feel powerless it makes us self-absorbed. How can we possibly be our best teacher selves when we are focused solely on ourselves? Hundreds of research studies found that when we are feeling powerless, we are more anxious; when we are anxious, we cannot get out of our own heads. This means we can't see things from another person's point of view (Cuddy, 2015, p. 122). As teachers, it is essential to be able to put ourselves in our students' shoes and to understand their perspectives and learning processes. The inability to empathize and step out of our own minds gets in our way to process what others are saying, and we literally can't understand what they are trying to share. This connection between anxiety and self-absorption is bidirectional, meaning you can begin with either part and it will create the other. If you are anxious, it will make you self-absorbed. If you are self-absorbed, it will make you more anxious. This self-focused lens does nothing to help us or our students.

When we teachers feel personally powerful, we can shift our focus from our teaching (ourselves) to our students' learning (others). This simple shift has a huge impact on students. I remember the first time I sat with my math coach after teaching a lesson that did not go so well. Half the class was able to figure out the problem, but the other half formed a line behind me and waited for me to one by one tell them what to do. During the debrief of the lesson, my coach asked me what I thought about the lesson. I began by explaining how I followed the math book's lesson plan and how I took all the steps. I told her what I did and why I did it. She smiled and listened and then asked me, "What about your students? What did you learn about them from today's lesson?" I was stumped by the question and simply said, "A lot of them needed my help." She followed up by saying, "And what else did you learn about why they needed you and what part they were confused about?" I had to admit that I didn't know. I broke down and told her, "I was so focused on following the steps of the lesson plan that I was not really paying attention to my students and their confusions." At the time, I did not know about Cuddy's research, but now I know that I was in a state of powerless anxiety that created a self-focus that seemed to blind me from really paying attention to my students.

The next week when my coach came back, I spoke with her before the lesson, and I explained that I wanted to focus more on my students and get out of my own head. She asked what would help me do that, and I said, "Well, I think I need to make it more fun and less intense. I get nervous when you are here, and then I stick too much to my plans, ignoring my students' in-the-moment needs." She cracked some joke about it being elementary math, and it made me laugh. She helped me realize I didn't have to make this lesson so high stakes. She reminded me of another lesson I did in the past that went really well. She was priming me for a sense of personal power as I remembered that past success. That day I do not know if I stuck to my lesson plan, but I do know that I focused much more on my students' needs, and it went a whole lot better.

One practice I now do when lesson planning is to zoom in on my students' experiences. I don't write, "Teacher will … and then teacher will…." Instead, I write, "Students will do … and then students will…." I focus on the students and what kinds of experiences they will be offered. Notice who you focus on when you plan and teach, and see if you may be suffering from the self-focus that anxiety brings. If you notice this, try priming yourself for personal power and then changing the way you plan so that it tells the story of what the students will be doing. This puts the spotlight on the students, where it belongs, and helps us be more impactful teachers.

Look at your teacher plans, and notice if they are focused mostly on what you will do. Try rewriting them here, focused on the student experience.

Connect the Dots

Remember those old-fashioned connect-the-dots worksheets where you would draw lines between each dot until a picture appeared? I sometimes feel like teaching practices and beliefs can become a series of dots, and if we don't connect them we don't get to see the whole picture. In one of Seth Godin's (2012) TED Talks he asks, "Are we asking kids to collect dots or connect dots? … We are really good at measuring how many dots they collect, but we teach virtually nothing about how to connect dots." When I heard this quote, I didn't just think about students; I also thought about us teachers. How often do we get the opportunity to make clear connections between our core beliefs and our daily practices? If we collect our beliefs and write them in pretty fonts and then plan our practices in an online planner but never build the cohesive ties between them, our core beliefs may end up never being lived. What follows are a few ways you can more consciously connect the dots between your teaching beliefs and practices.

First, go back and revisit the core beliefs you created from Chapter 2. Look at them with fresh eyes, and reflect on whether or how you may want to make any revisions. I tend to revise mine at least once a year and sometimes much more frequently. Next, look at your teaching planner that lists your daily practices and look for connections. Ask yourself, "Do my teaching practices align with my beliefs? Which ones?" Finally, look for gaps and discrepancies, and don't gloss over them. If you have been collecting practices like dots but not connecting them, then this is the time to make some different choices. Reflect on some possible next steps based on what you find. One example follows.

> If we collect our beliefs and write them in pretty fonts and then plan our practices in online planners but never build the cohesive ties between them, our core beliefs may end up never being lived.

Core Beliefs	Teaching Practices	Connections or Disconnections	Reflection and Next Steps
Experiencing joyful reading leads to more engaged and lifelong readers.	Offer choices so students self-select much of what they read.	*Clear Connection:* When students get to choose what they want to read, they enjoy it so much more than being forced to read only what others assign. Plus, they are much more likely to actually read.	How can students be more helpful for one another's reading joy? Add in book talks and recommendations. Give them some time to talk about their books in class.
Students benefit from building self-confidence through lots of practice and feedback.	Give weekly quizzes on the chapters students were assigned in a class novel.	*Disconnection:* Because many students did not really read the chapters, their grades did nothing to create self-confidence as readers. It either reinforced that SparkNotes work or that all that matters with reading is a score at the end of the week.	What if I gave students some time in school to read what they chose? This would give them time to actually practice and get feedback and help from me.

Use the following form to try this yourself.

Core Beliefs	Teaching Practices	Connections or Disconnections	Reflection and Next Steps

---

Your Personal Power

⭐ Prime yourself for feeling powerful.

⭐ Don't make every day game day.

⭐ It's not all about me.

⭐ Connect the dots.

VIEW STUDENT LEARNING AS A PRACTICE

If it helps us teachers to have a sense of personal power, then it will also help our students to feel the same when it comes to learning. When they are anxious and feel powerless, they can't use their executive functioning skills or listen and learn from others. We can use the same practices with our students that help us feel more powerful as teachers.

Teach Students How to Prime

We can teach our students how to prime their brains for powerful feelings. This means we explain and model for them how to remember a past experience of power and success as well as teach them what personal power means. We can begin our classes by having students remember back to a successful previous learning experience and share it with a partner. Or we may ask students to keep a journal of moments when they experienced personal power that they can refer back to whenever they want to flip the switch on their feelings. In fact, while our students prime themselves for learning, we can do our own priming practice for our teaching. Everyone can then enter class with a can-do mindset.

Vary Students' Types of Practice

We can make sure we are not making each day feel like game day and create spaces for students to do different types of practice. We can try to reduce our students' anxiety so they can focus on our lessons, the texts' information, and their classmates' ideas. When our students feel powerful, they can show up ready to learn and engage with a belief that they will be able to learn and grow. Look at your lesson and unit plans, and code them for the types of practice you are offering your students. Do they have time for repetitive practice, original practice, mindful practice, and playful practice? If you notice certain types of practice getting all the time and energy, make a plan for offering other experiences to your students.

Help Students Make Connections

Looking at how our core beliefs and practices connect or don't is not just for teachers but also important for students. Regularly offer students time to examine their learning practices alongside their core beliefs. What connections are they making? Where are they seeing disconnections? At the midpoint and end of each curricular unit, there are opportunities for this sort of reflection. When students do experience success, ask them to look at the practices that led to this success. By connecting results to the process, it helps students develop what Carol Dweck (2007) calls a growth mindset. The same can be said of less successful experiences. Help students reflect on what practices did or did not lead to the outcome.

Viewing Student Learning as a Practice

★ Teach students how to prime.

★ Vary students' types of practice.

★ Help students make connections.

A TEACHING PRACTICE

In this chapter, we learned about the different types of practice we may choose to take on as teachers and how we can practice aligning our core beliefs to our teaching from a place of personal power. In essence, this chapter helps us view our teaching not as a job or as a skill to be mastered but as a series of practices we can choose each day. Just like I don't *do* yoga, I have a yoga practice, I encourage us all to speak about, think about, and write about our teaching from this same viewpoint. I have a teaching practice. By viewing your teaching as a practice, it frees you up to be original, mindful, and playful. It helps you feel less pressure, and it helps you be more of your true teacher self. This perspective allows you to stand in your own personal power. The next time you are at a dinner party and someone asks you what you do, I suggest you respond by proudly saying, "I have a teaching practice." But then be prepared for a much longer conversation where you might have to explain what that means.

BUILD
BALANCED RELATIONSHIPS

4

Video 4

Source: One 21 Productions

As we let our own light shine, we … give other people permission to do the same.
As we're liberated from our own fear, our presence automatically liberates others.

—Marianne Williamson

One of my all-time favorite children's book series is the *Frog and Toad* series by Arnold Lobel. My husband and I love these characters so much that the readings at our wedding came from the books. One of the many aspects I adore about these stories is the realistic way Lobel portrays relationships. Take, for example, the story "The Hat" (Lobel, 2004). Frog gives Toad a hat for his birthday, and it is much too big for his head. When Frog tries to take the gift back, Toad says absolutely not; he wants to keep it and use it because his beloved friend gave it to him. But Toad spends the rest of his birthday tripping and bumping into things as he wears the hat that is much too large for him. At the end of the day, Frog suggests that Toad spend his night dreaming and thinking big thoughts so his head will grow and fit into the hat. That night as Toad sleeps, Frog sneaks into his room, takes the hat, pours water over it, and puts it in a warm place so it will shrink. The next morning when Toad puts on his hat, it fits. Toad is thrilled that his present now works, and Frog gets to relish in his friend's happiness.

When I read this story, I notice so many qualities of healthy relationships. First, I notice how important both giving and receiving are to these two friends. They invest in each other's happiness. I also notice how gratitude and generosity are at the forefront. Then I notice how there is space for each of these two friends to be who they are, which is quite different from each other.

As teachers, we can learn so much from these two fictional characters and how they not only navigate challenges together but also complement and support one another, working as a team.

CONNECTION IS A BASIC HUMAN NEED

Psychologists have been studying connection and our human need for relationships for a very long time, and with the rise of positive psychology, there have been so many findings in the past few decades. I want to highlight a few key findings and how they may affect teachers. Self-determination theory, developed by Deci and Ryan (2000), focuses on the three main types of motivation—(1) competence, (2) relatedness, and (3) autonomy. While all three are important, let's focus on relatedness here, which deals with the desire to interact with, be connected to, and experience caring for other people. Through our daily interactions with people, we seek this feeling of belongingness. We must feel we relate and belong with others in our community because one of our basic needs is to have close relationships with others. This makes me think that having solid lesson plans and high test scores is not really the full picture of what it means to be an effective teacher. We also need to feel that we belong to the larger school community.

> Having solid lesson plans and high test scores is not really the full picture of what it means to be an effective teacher.

Seligman, considered a father of positive psychology, developed the PERMA model for explaining well-being. PERMA stands for *positive emotion, engagement, relationships, meaning,* and *accomplishments*. His research claims that when we maximize each of these elements our sense of well-being increases—something he calls authentic happiness. If we just zoom in on relationships, the research shows that humans are social animals that thrive on connection and positive interactions with others. We rely on these connections when our lives become challenging. In fact, we now know that feeling a lack of connection can actually cause us pain. Feeling isolated from others has been tested with fMRI machines and shown to activate the same areas of the brain as physical pain (Cuddy, 2015; Eisenberger, Lieberman, & Williams, 2003; Prinstein, 2015). Professor Prinstein explains that this is because from an evolutionary perspective, isolation from others would have been the worst thing for our survival as a species (Prinstein, 2015). As teachers, it will improve our well-being in school to build strong connections with our colleagues and students to avoid the pain of isolation and to have support systems when we are handling challenges. Two main ways we can form these essential connections are through building trust and learning to listen well.

Focus on Trust

Cuddy's (2015) research shows the importance of how we show up for others, which she defines as "how we approach the people we hope to connect with and influence" (p. 71). Her team found that the two most important aspects of how we show up and are perceived by others are warmth and competence. Cuddy doesn't define warmth outright and uses the terms *trust* and *warmth* interchangeably. I think of warmth as a feeling you create by genuinely wanting to know the other person, accept them as they are, and show that you care about them. In other words, we ask these questions: Can I trust this person? Can I respect this person? While competence might seem like an obvious quality to look for in others, their research actually found that warmth was more important than competence when it comes to building relationships. Cuddy (2015) explains it this way:

> Why do we prioritize warmth over competence? Because from an evolutionary perspective, it is more crucial to our survival to know whether a person deserves our trust. If he doesn't, we'd better keep our distance, because he's potentially dangerous, especially if he is competent. We do value people who are capable, especially in circumstances where the trait is necessary, but we only notice that *after* we've judged their trustworthiness. (p. 72)

When I read this research, I went through my memories of relationships and realized that this finding did ring personally true. I can think of several times in my career when I met a brilliant person who seemed to know so much, yet I did not trust the person and therefore couldn't form any real and lasting relationship with them. I also worked with novice teachers who were still forming their expertise as teachers, yet I trusted them completely, and these were collaborative experiences where I thrived.

Learn to Really Listen

Cuddy's research also found that when we listen to others it forms the kind of strong relationships we are looking for. She quotes Ury, who says, "When we listen to someone, it's the most profound act of human respect" (Cuddy, 2015, p. 76). In fact, her team claims there are five positive outcomes from learning to talk less and listen more. First, they found that people trust you. Second, they found that you acquire useful information, which makes it easier for you to solve problems. Third, they found that you begin to see other people as individuals and maybe even allies. Fourth, you develop solutions that other people are willing to accept and even adopt. Fifth, when people feel heard, they are more willing to listen, which creates a healthy reciprocity (p. 81).

When I think back to all of my less-than-ideal relationships, I can now see how often one or likely both of us were not really listening. One example that comes to mind right away was during a department meeting years ago. The principal, my colleagues, and I were meeting because we could not agree on a change in the summer reading program that some of us wanted to make. In fact, this "conversation" had been going on for weeks, and we were all digging our heels into our own camp. To this day, about a decade later, I could tell you my main points, but if I am honest, I don't recall anyone else's. This is because while they were talking I was defending and arguing my side either out loud or in my mind. While I am not proud of this lack of listening, I am human, and we all can fall into this habit at times. That meeting, like all the others around this topic, ended with winners and losers and many unhappy teachers. But when I look back now, I realize what we lost was not just an argument but a sense of trust and warmth between us. We never did repair that part of our relationship that year. Reading Cuddy's research, I now know the solution to our dilemma was so simple in theory but challenging in practice—trying to listen from a place of wondering what it was like to be in the other person's shoes. We'll come back to this topic of listening later in the chapter, when I offer some relationship practices we can implement.

Connection Is a Basic Human Need

★ Focus on trust by being trustworthy and showing others how much you care about them.

★ Learn to really listen and practice this skill with friends, colleagues, and students.

Try paying attention to how you listen and if you are getting all five benefits from learning to talk less and listen more. In what ways do you want to grow as a listener?

THE WHOLE PICTURE OF PROFESSIONAL RELATIONSHIPS

While it can sometimes feel tempting to close our classroom doors, eat lunch in our classrooms, and avoid shared spaces, when we operate as islands our effectiveness can suffer. It takes energy and time to build balanced relationships, but in the long run the research is clear on why the energy is worth it. Let's look at four main types of relationships—with ourselves, our colleagues, our students, and their families—and what we know about why each one makes us a stronger and better teacher.

Build Relationships With Ourselves

Even though it can be easy to skip over this first type of relationship, how we view ourselves affects all of our other relationships. Think about the last time you felt insecure about a choice you made and how that influenced that parent meeting, or the time you felt confident with your students' work and how that spilled over into your next team meeting. How we view and relate to ourselves is our most primary relationship and where we want to look first when building balanced relationships with others.

The research on how we view ourselves is what Bandura (1977) calls self-efficacy. Self-efficacy is "the conviction that one can successfully execute the behavior required to produce outcomes" (Bandura, 1977, p. 193). We might colloquially call this self-confidence. Do we believe we can be successful in our work each day? If we go back to the reflection we did in Chapter 2 around our core beliefs and in Chapter 3 on our teaching practices, then self-efficacy asks us to look at our attitude about whether we think we can actually succeed in implementing practices that match our core beliefs. Teacher self-efficacy is a teacher's sense of competence (Protheroe, 2008, p. 53).

> Self-efficacy asks us to look at our attitude about whether we think we can actually succeed in implementing practices that match our core beliefs.

In my experience, teacher self-efficacy is more like a continuum than a box to check off. Some days I feel super confident in my ability, and other days or periods I am filled with self-doubt. One way I expose my current relationship toward my teaching ability is to pay attention to my self-talk. What am I saying to myself? Is it nice? Is it fair? Is it accurate? For example, during my first year of teaching science, I recall the thoughts I was saying to myself as my eighth period students walked into the classroom. I recall thinking, "You are never going to get through this. They are going to ignore you and talk over you. You are failing them. They are learning nothing from you." I berated myself until it was time to start teaching, and guess what? They did talk over me a lot of the time, and I did not get through most of my lesson plans. The issue was twofold, though. One, I was not effectively engaging this class. Two, I was forming a negative and self-defeating relationship with myself.

In order to change the dynamic of the class, I first had to change my dynamic with myself. I ended up seeking help from my mentor and changing up my lesson plans, so I was being proactive on the lesson-planning front. But, equally important, I changed the ways I spoke to myself about my teaching. It was forced at first, but I began to give myself positive pep talks about how I was going to be as a teacher. Rather than saying to myself, "You are failing them," I would say, "You got this. You can connect with these students. You are a good teacher." By not only changing my lesson approach but also changing my self-talk, I was building more teacher self-efficacy, which ended up helping me not just with that one class period but across my teaching career.

Build Relationships With Colleagues

A large part of being a teacher is also being on a team. Some teams feel unified and successful, and other teams can feel like a bunch of individuals who happen to be on the same field. Recent research by John Hattie (2016) found that teachers who share a sense of collective teacher efficacy have the biggest impact on student achievement. Collective teacher efficacy means that teachers in a school carry an attitude that together they can make a difference for students (Donohoo, 2016). This is ranked as the top factor influencing student achievement with an effect size of 1.57 (Hattie, 2016). Despite outside factors such as students' family background and resources, when groups of teachers come together believing they can affect student learning, they often do.

> When groups of teachers come together believing they can affect student learning, they often do.

When teachers have strong and trusting relationships with one another, they can practice the kinds of behaviors that promote collective teacher efficacy. For example, it helps when teachers are part of learning networks because they make connections and share professional knowledge and strategies with one another. Hargreaves and Fullan (2012) explain that "some of the most powerful, underutilized strategies in all of education involve the deliberate use of teamwork—enabling teachers to learn from each other within and across schools—and building cultures and networks of communication, learning, trust, and collaboration around the team as well" (p. 89). While many school leaders, instructional coaches, and professional development consultants lead peer-to-peer learning initiatives, some of the most powerful teamwork experiences I have seen have been initiated by teachers for teachers.

One high school where I have the privilege of supporting teachers uses the pineapple chart, which is an informal way of inviting their colleagues into their classrooms (Gonzalez, 2016). Let me give you a bit of background about this high school. There are between 1,600 and 1,800 students who attend this school each day because of a huge transiency issue. There are over 150 teachers who work full time and several dozen part-time teachers. Since a department might have over 25 teachers, it is virtually impossible to free them up for common planning and meeting times during the school day. The teachers took this collaboration problem and ran with it. Two teachers read about the pineapple chart model where each week a chart is posted with a box for each period. Teachers can sign up by putting their names in the box and the topic of the lesson to show they are opening up their classroom for their colleagues to come in. They also hang paper pineapples in the classroom doorway as a signal that they are open for visitors.

While it took some time to build momentum, and at first the same handful of teachers opened up their classrooms, after a few months it gained traction. Now in the second year of their initiative, more than half of the faculty have volunteered to be a visited classroom. The entire culture of the building has changed. Teachers are excited to share ideas, they know each other better, and the students' test scores have gone up. Even though the pineapple itself is a kitschy idea, it has served as a team mascot. Teachers have pineapple notebooks, pineapple sticky notes, and a few even have pineapple clothing. When I get the chance to go collaborate with these teachers, what strikes me most is not just that teacher practice has changed but also that the belief system has changed. Teachers work together as a team and believe that they can make a difference.

Another way to view the success with this high school's pineapple chart initiative is through the lens of professional capital. Hargreaves and Fullan (2012) cite studies conducted by Leana (2011) in 130 New York City schools. One aspect the research team measured was social capital—to what extent do teachers in this school work in a trusting, collaborative way to focus on learning and the engagement and improvement of student achievement? They found that schools with high social capital showed positive achievement outcomes. "Being in a school around others who are working effectively rubs off on teachers and engages them" (Hargreaves & Fullan, 2012, p. 37). I don't think the teachers at the large high school had enough opportunities to have their hard work rub off on one another until they began visiting each other's classrooms. This, in turn, created more opportunities for professional conversations, which led to more teamwork and confidence.

Build Relationships With Students

When we have strong, positive relationships with our students, they show up more engaged to learn and end up more successful as learners in our classes. This is seen in everyday interactions with students and also in the research on student voice. The Quaglia Student Voice Survey (2016) shows that "students who feel cared for as individuals by their teachers are also more likely to engage in pro-academic behaviors. Such students are three times more likely to report putting forth their best effort, working hard to reach their goals, and pushing themselves to do better academically than are peers who do not report believing teachers care" (p. 67). Reeve (2002) claims that student motivation is in part a result of student and teacher relationships. Teacher credibility, an outcome of student and teacher relationships, is one of John Hattie's (2016) top qualities for effective instruction, with a 0.9 effect size. Unfortunately, of the students surveyed in the Quaglia studies, only 55 percent believed their teachers cared about them as individuals.

Students learn more and better from teachers they like and connect with. If we know this to be true, then it can be tempting to be the "fun" teacher or the "cool" teacher who makes the curriculum easy and tries to be friends with students. There is a very distinct line between being a friend and being friendly. We also know that when we have high expectations for our students they raise their own expectations for themselves. So our job is not to be our students' friends but to connect with our students, to get to know them and their goals, and to create an environment where everyone feels safe to learn.

We can build strong student relationships in some of the same ways we can connect with ourselves and our colleagues. It helps to look at our beliefs about our students and the ways we talk about them in our heads and out loud. Shifting from negative to positive talk makes a huge difference. We can also learn to listen to our students and create time and space to hear their ideas and reflections. Trust is built when we are clear and share our own learning processes and stories with them. When we show up more authentically as ourselves, it helps students do the same.

I'll never forget a student in my class from early in my teaching career. Chelsea was a tall, lanky girl who literally stood out from her classmates. She spent the previous years in a self-contained special education class, and the year with me was her first year in an inclusive classroom. Chelsea rolled her eyes at me when I gave directions. She put her head in her arms and pretended to nap during independent work time. When I asked her to share her work, she almost always refused. I just was not sure how to connect with her.

> Our job is not to be our students' friends, but it is our job to connect with our students, to get to know them and their goals, and to create an environment where everyone feels safe to learn.

One afternoon I asked her if she wanted to stay in during recess to help me and a few other classmates organize the classroom library. It had become a mess, and my typical student volunteers wanted to clean it up. She accepted the invitation to help us out. The next day when it was time for recess she asked if she could clean my blackboards (yes, I am dating myself that I had blackboards). The day after that, she asked if I had any papers to organize. It got to the point that I was worried she would never get recess again. So instead of helping at recess, she stayed after school a few days a week for about fifteen minutes to help me clean, organize, or on some days to just sit there and read. We didn't talk that much. When I asked her questions, she gave me one-word answers, but she kept showing up each day.

As the year went on, she didn't put her head down to nap as often, and she only rolled her eyes at me half as many times as before. At the end of the school year, I was still not sure that Chelsea had gotten what she needed from me. All I knew was that I didn't give up on her, I never spoke about her negatively, I listened when she did speak, and I was always there for her when she needed space to just be. On the first day of school the following year, Chelsea came up to me at the end of the day and handed me an envelope and ran away. When I opened the envelope, there was a card inside where she wrote, "Thank you Ms. Goldberg." I cried when I read it. Chelsea went on to more and more success each year and eventually no longer qualified for special education services because of her strong performance. She taught me the power of student and teacher relationships, and I am still thankful for having the privilege of being her teacher, even though I learned just as much from her.

Build Relationships With Families

Trying to connect with myself, my colleagues, and my students can seem like the full picture, but students' families are also important when it comes to building relationships. My friend and colleague Kerrie Larosa, who is a parent coach and social worker, collaborates with me when it comes to helping teachers create strong home and school connections. During our collaboration, we came across some research on the current status of school and home communication, and the findings are not that promising. Sixty percent of families in the United States report not receiving a phone call about their child from an administrator or teacher in the preceding year (Noel, Stark, Redford, & Zukerberg, 2013). Sixty-six percent of families of secondary-age students do not agree that teachers keep them informed about classroom activities, events, and requirements (National School Public Relations Association, 2011). Less than 25 percent of parents can name a basic milestone that their child learned in school in the previous year (Public Agenda, 2012). It is important to note that this research is all based on the reporting of families and not from teachers. Regardless of whether teachers are doing more than these studies show, the trends are clear that most parents who are surveyed did not feel like true partners with their children's teachers. What we do know is that when teachers are confident in their own abilities and effectiveness, they are more likely to welcome parental participation (Donohoo, 2016, p. 25).

During my collaboration with Kerrie Larosa, we found several key factors that both teachers and parents could use to help forge stronger home and school connections. These include a willingness to participate, trust, communication, mutual respect, collaboration, and shared vested interest, as well as being teammates, making positive assumptions, and having realistic expectations. When beginning a partnership with a student's family or trying to repair a slightly damaged relationship, it helps to begin with rapport-building practices. First, find something common that you both want for the student. Then, go out of your way to communicate positive experiences to parents when you see them happening. When an issue does arise, it is so helpful to meet in person, face to face, so you can talk as teammates about how you can both support the student more.

Early in my teaching career, I got great advice from my mentor. She suggested I call each student's home and introduce myself to the families and share something I loved about their child. I took the advice and called two students' parents a day for the first few weeks of the school year. Almost every single parent was surprised to get a call from the teacher. Then the surprise turned to fear: What had their child done wrong? I had to reassure them that nothing was wrong and that I was calling to share something positive. The fear turned to gratitude. That year, I had great parent participation and had some days when there were almost as many volunteers as students in the classroom. When there were issues, we were able to tackle them together as teammates because we had started off on the right foot. Making time for positive parent relationships from the start has always served me and my students well, as they can see we are all on the same team.

The Whole Picture of Professional Relationships

★ Build relationships with ourselves.

★ Build relationships with colleagues.

★ Build relationships with students.

★ Build relationships with families.

Consider all of the types of relationships, and reflect on which ones you think you could focus more attention on.

RELATIONSHIP-BUILDING PRACTICES

Now that we understand just how essential strong and supportive relationships are, let's examine and try out a few practices that can help us become better at creating them. It is clear that in order for relationships to thrive, there needs to be attention, purpose, and emotional understanding. Some key practices that support these relationships include shared celebrations, dialogue, and finding the right balance.

Shared Celebrations

When the people in our lives share news with us, especially good news, our relationships can be strengthened or weakened based on how we respond: "Our ability to respond enthusiastically to good news in a relationship is more important than how we communicate with each other during bad times" (Greenville-Cleave, 2012, p. 48). This finding is a bit surprising until the four types of responses are examined and then it does start to make sense. Research conducted by Gable, Reis, Impett, and Asher (2004) found four main styles when responding to good news in a relationship.

- *Passive constructive responses:* You respond in an unenthusiastic way.

- *Passive destructive responses:* You respond by turning the conversation back to yourself.

- *Active destructive responses:* You have a negative response and actively squelch their good news.

- *Active constructive responses*: You offer enthusiastic and unbridled support.

After reading this list, it is likely not surprising that the only suggested way to respond is the active constructive response because it is the only way that shows your support and makes the person feel better about their news.

Choose Your Responses

One practice we can all begin today is to pay attention to how we respond when the people in our professional lives share good news with us. Notice your body language as well as what you say and how you say it. Also, recognize that not everybody is comfortable with lots of praise and instead may prefer active constructive responses that are more subtle, like asking questions that show you are interested. The following list can help you hone this practice:

- Smile and nod.

- Give your full and undivided attention.

- Speak in an enthusiastic and excited manner.

- Share encouragement and excitement.

- Ask questions about the good news.

- Be genuine.

Check Your Ratio

Another research finding that helps build strong relationships entails the positivity ratio of your interactions. John Gottman (2017) studies why some couples stay happily married and others divorce. While I realize this book is not about married couples, the findings do relate to other types of close relationships like the ones we have with our close colleagues and students. Gottman (2017) found that in order to create happy relationships there needs to be a 5:1 ratio of positive to negative interactions. This means that for every negative interaction there needs to be five positive ones. He clarifies that negative interactions are not just ones where one person gets angry but specifically ones where it is expressed along with criticism, contempt, or defensiveness. His research suggests the following behaviors that promote positive interactions:

- Be interested.

- Demonstrate the other person matters.

- Show intentional appreciation.

- Find opportunities for agreement.

- Empathize and apologize.

- Accept the other person's perspective.

- Make jokes.

Gottman's (2017) website suggests "take it upon yourself to create more positive interactions in your relationship, and also try to notice the small moments of positivity that currently exist there, and that you may have been missing."

Perform Acts of Kindness

We have all been told how important it is to be a kind person because, well, it is the right thing to do. But there is also research that supports the idea that when we are kind to others it creates happiness, and that happiness becomes contagious: "People's happiness depends on the happiness of others with whom they are connected" (Grenville-Cleave, 2012, p. 46). Studies have found that if a friend of yours lives within a mile of your home and they become happier, it will increase the probability of your own happiness by 25 percent. Wow! Imagine how we can affect one another when our classrooms are right next door to one another. The wonderful thing about performing acts of kindness is that they don't cost anything. Writing a thank-you note, making extra copies for a colleague, and giving a hug all show you care and take very little time.

Recently I was working alongside some teachers during a multiday professional development workshop series in their school. At the end of the series, they presented me with a cupcake and card to say thank you. That little gesture made me happy and feel appreciated; in turn, it spread to all of us in that room. As we ended our session, each person got up and spontaneously hugged each other and thanked each other for their collaborations.

> For every negative interaction, there needs to be five positive ones.

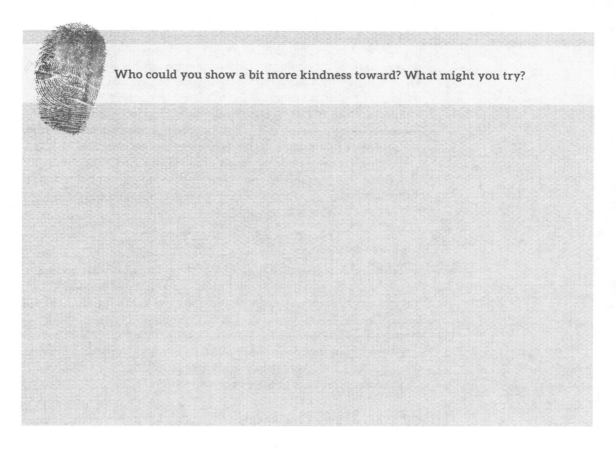

Who could you show a bit more kindness toward? What might you try?

Choose to Dialogue

Let's recall the earlier part of this chapter when we examined the bene-fits of listening to others. When we listen, we have the opportunity to build stronger relationships and to gain new perspectives. Scientist and writer David Bohm (2004) beautifully describes the importance of under-standing what true dialogue entails and how we can more often enter these sorts of spaces. Drawing on global, political, and religious disagree-ments, Bohm explains that we have a misunderstanding of what true dia-logue entails. He explains, "In a dialogue, each person does not attempt to make common certain ideas or items of information that are already known to him. Rather, it may be said that the two people are making something in common, i.e., creating something together that is new" (p. 3). What would it look like if we approached our colleagues, our students, and their families with the goal of creating something new together? This sounds like true teamwork. For example, inviting parents in to plan an event together or using grade-level team meeting time to create a whole new unit of study together. It is not just about what you are creating but the focus on creating it together that makes the difference.

The question, of course, is how do we do that? Bohm (2004) answers, "We need to be able to communicate freely in a creative movement in which no one permanently holds to or otherwise defends his own ideas" (p. 4). We often enter into conversations with a set of steadfast beliefs and see the goal as getting the other person to see things our way. This is not true dialogue because in this case there are winners and losers, and how could strong relationships grow from someone feeling like they lost? Instead, we can realize that "dialogue is something more of a common participation, in which we are not playing a game against each other, but with each other. In dialogue, everyone wins" (p. 7). The way everyone wins is if the dialogue leads to a co-creation of ideas that everyone contributed to. Let's think about how to put this into practice.

Set Intentions

Before you can enter a dialogue, it helps to know this is what you want. Simply deciding to talk to someone else—a colleague, a student, or a parent—does not mean you are set up to be in dialogue. If your intention is to convince, defend, or persuade, then you are likely not choosing dialogue and may be looking for a debate or an argument. If your intention is to solve a problem, work collaboratively, or create something original, then dialogue will likely help you. Be honest with yourself about what sort of communication you are choosing to have.

Get Clear on Your Own Beliefs

Part of being in productive dialogue is to get clear on your own beliefs. This is not for the purpose of being able to prove your side but instead helps you to know what you are bringing with you to the communication. I find it helpful to journal or list my beliefs so I can examine them on the page. You have already done some of this work in Chapter 2. You may want to go back to some of those practices with a more specific topic or lens in mind where you know you want to be in dialogue with others. Know yourself and what you are bringing with you and also how open you are to having your mind changed. For example, you may want to list some of the beliefs and then rate how open you are to alternative ideas next to them.

In the example that follows, I was preparing for a schoolwide faculty meeting with my colleagues about the role of homework in our curriculum. I wanted to enter the meeting with awareness of what I already believed so I could be in dialogue (see opposite page).

Listen With Empathy

It can be so darn challenging to go into a dialogue choosing to listen to alternative beliefs from our own. This requires us to be open enough

Dialogue Topic: Homework		
My Beliefs:	**How Open Am I?**	
	Closed	**Open**
Homework has no place in elementary school.	X	
Homework should mostly be chosen by students.		X
Busywork should never be homework.	X	
Choice reading is acceptable homework.		X

List Beliefs and Reflect on Openness

to desire to know how another person views the same situation. While I am not talking about bringing up politics at the Thanksgiving dinner table—something I would never recommend—I am talking about seeking to better understand the worldview of the people who see the world very differently than we do. Seth Godin (2017a) has this phenomenal blog post called "Everyone Else Is Irrational," where he writes this:

> Everyone else makes bad decisions, is shortsighted, prejudiced, subject to whims, temper tantrums, outbursts and short-term thinking.
>
> Once you see it that way, it's easier to remember ...
>
> that we're everyone too.

What Godin has taught me in this blog post and as one of my mentors in his altMBA workshop is that when we use empathy we are not necessarily agreeing with the person's choices but we are understanding why they make the choices they do based on what they see and believe.

Let me break that down a bit. First, can we agree that we are all irrational, meaning none of us makes rational decisions 100 percent of the time? Then, can we step back and ask ourselves questions about what the other person has experienced in the world and has been taught to believe that has created their current worldview? For example, I often ask myself, "What does this person see here?" and "How is this person framing the experience?" and "What values and experiences are they bringing into this current choice?" Simply by asking some questions, I am bringing some empathy to the dialogue because I am trying to understand the other person and not just make them wrong. I'd like to share one example of how this changed my entire relationship with a colleague.

> When we use empathy we are not necessarily agreeing with the person's choices, but we are understanding why they make the choices they do based on what they see and believe.

For almost a year, I was sitting cross-armed in department meetings, arguing my side of the situation, and then continuing to fight with my colleague Amy in my head all afternoon, including my drive home from work. I couldn't get Amy out of my mind. It was like she moved in and I was going to need to argue with her every day until I won or gave up. This was not only a total waste of time, since Amy was not even really there, but also she had so much power over my life, because she was following me into my downtime. I have shared this story with other teacher friends and found that all of them could relate to this idea that we spin our wheels having mental arguments with people in our minds, leading us to be more angry, less open, and emotionally charged up.

One day I asked Amy to meet with me one on one because I was exhausted from our rather toxic relationship dynamic. I really wanted to find a way to collaborate and to get her out of my head. We sat down and talked about our own schooling experiences as students and what led us to become teachers. When Amy shared her story, I leaned in and really listened. I genuinely wanted to know her better. She explained that she was the first person in her family to attend college, and she was proud of this achievement. Then she went on to tell me that during her first semester in college she was called to her English professor's office to go over her paper. Apparently, the professor had given her a D and marked up her paper with all sorts of red marks. Then he turned to her and said, "Where did you go to high school? They obviously did not prepare you for college writing." Amy shed a tear telling me this story about an experience from twenty-five years earlier in her life. She went on to explain to me, "When I became a teacher, I vowed I would never have a single one of my students leave my class unprepared for college. I never want another person to feel the shame that I felt. This is why I am so hard on my students. I correct every single mistake. They need to learn now so they don't end up sitting in a professor's office humiliated."

Amy's story had a profound impact on me. Because she trusted me enough to tell me that story, I felt closer to her, and I also had a much clearer idea about why she made the choices she did in her classroom. Even though I believed she was turning her students off writing and focusing so much on mistakes that she missed their writing gems, I now understood and really empathized with her rationale. She was making her choices from a place of wanting to protect and help her students. Up until hearing her story, I had no idea this was her true intention. Now that I understood her worldview a bit more, I could collaborate with her so we could find strategies we both agreed helped students learn to be stronger writers, ready for college, and also confident and enthusiastic without being beaten down. What shifted our relationship was one dialogue where I sought to understand her worldview and how she was, in fact, making choices that were more rational than they first seemed to be from an outside perspective.

Whose worldview do you want to better understand? What questions might you ask them? How might you listen with even more empathy?

Relationship-Building Practices

★ Create shared celebrations.

- Choose your responses.
- Check your ratio.
- Perform acts of kindness.

★ Choose to dialogue.

- Set intentions.
- Get clear on your own beliefs.
- Listen with empathy.

FIND BALANCE

As I wrap up this chapter, I find myself thinking back to the concept of balance. One of my teachers, Pat, said that balance is the ability to move in any direction. At first I was not clear on what she meant as it relates to relationships. The more I thought, the more I realized that when relationships with ourselves or others are less than optimal it feels like there are roadblocks and blind spots so that we actually can't move in that direction. If I am upset with a colleague, I might avoid walking by her classroom, or if I am beating myself up with negative self-talk, I am often putting up barriers to what I believe I can change and be. Those barriers and blocks prevent me from teaching fully as myself. If I am honest with myself, so much of my teaching that feels artificial and inauthentic is created by relationships that make me feel I just can't move in a direction that seems right to me. So even though the practices in this chapter can sometimes feel tangential to teaching and learning, I urge you to look more closely at your relationships and consider where you feel stuck. Those are the places and people to work with first.

DRIVE
PROFESSIONAL GROWTH

Video 5

Source: One 21 Production

Whatever makes you uncomfortable is your biggest opportunity for growth.

—Bryant McGill

When I was six years old, I would play school. I lined up my stuffed animals in a row, put worksheets in front of them, and wrote letters and numbers on the blackboard my dad hung in my playroom. I used my red pen to correct brown bear's paper and made a smiley face on my Cabbage Patch Kid's ditto sheet. I was mimicking what I thought being a teacher entailed.

Years later as a senior in high school, my English teacher gave us the challenge of an I-Search project. We chose a project of personal interest and used a combination of firsthand research and reading books on the topic to become an expert (this was pre-Internet). It was personalized learning decades before that term was popularized. I chose to do my research on a new method called Writing Workshop, which I had heard about from my boyfriend's little brother, Sam, who was in first grade. I contacted Sam's teacher and asked if I could observe in her classroom during Writing Workshop. This was my first real step in driving my professional growth, and I was not even a real teacher yet. It would be another year until I was enrolled in a teacher education program and a few more after that when I could call myself a real-life professional teacher, but as a seventeen-year-old I wanted to learn all I could to prepare for my future.

As I stepped into that first-grade classroom, I watched as twenty or so students sat quietly and wrote on paper with extra-large lines. I watched as each one chose something that mattered to them and tried their best to write the words that captured it. Then I sat down next to the teacher who was conferring with writers, and I listened as she gave each student feedback. What struck me immediately was how different this teacher was than what I imagined a teacher really did. She had no red pens, and she was not there to correct her students' writing. She was listening openly, asking questions, and then showing examples of what other writers did that may help them. This was my first real dose of professional learning from the other side of the desk.

At the end of the day, I stayed late and asked that teacher dozens of questions about what she was doing and why. After a while, she smiled and asked if I wanted to borrow her copy of the book *The Art of Teaching Writing,* by Lucy Calkins (1994). I nodded yes and went straight home to get started. I took so many notes that I think I wrote more about that professional book than Lucy herself wrote. When I went back the next week, I asked if I could try leading a writing conference based on what I read.

A decade later, after getting experience as a classroom teacher, I was hired by Lucy Calkins to work as a staff developer at the Teachers College Reading and Writing Project. And while I was so thrilled to have this career opportunity, I was even more excited about the chance to learn with the best teachers in the world. I look back now and realize that my thirst for professional growth started all the way back when I was a teenager and has never wavered. I just wish I could go back to my six-year-old self and tell her to put down that red pen and to sit next to brown bear and help him be a better writer. Luckily I was able to find my senior year English teacher a few years ago and thank her for offering me the opportunity for personalized learning that propelled my teaching journey.

A lot has changed since the 1990s in terms of what is available for professional growth opportunities, and while visiting other teachers' classrooms and reading professional books are still high on my list, there are so many other ways we teachers can continue to learn and grow together. In this chapter, I highlight a few of the main ways teachers today drive their professional growth.

LEAN INTO AREAS FOR GROWTH

If we go back to Chapter 2 where we named our core beliefs, we can begin to consider the ways we want to grow more fully into them. Even when I can name my beliefs and have tried to connect them to my teaching practices, I know there is often more to explore and more to develop. But it can be challenging to keep up with the daily demands of teaching along with putting some time and effort into myself. We can ask these questions: What are my areas for growth? What do I want to learn? What do I need to know and be able to do in order to really live my beliefs? If we don't prioritize our own learning alongside our students' then we are not modeling what it means to be a lifelong learner, and we are not actively seeking to teach like the best version of ourselves. What follows is a list of characteristics that have served teachers well as they seek to discover their own areas for growth.

- We set goals for ourselves and not just our students.

- We say yes to every learning opportunity available that aligns with our core beliefs.

- We take risks and try out new approaches that match our beliefs.

- We acknowledge what we don't yet know how to do.

- We reflect on what is and is not working for this particular group of students.

- We lean into the struggle of trying something new.

- We hold on to what does work.

- We ask for help from others.

- We offer help to others.

When you read this list, you likely noticed that there are a bunch of verbs here. Growth involves action. It doesn't just happen on its own. Growth requires us to lean in and seek it. I also think of professional growth as a journey. It is not staying in the exact same place each day; rather, it is going into new territories to see what I may find. The broadcaster Andy Rooney said, "Everyone wants to live on top of the mountain, but all the happiness and growth occur while you are climbing it." I totally agree and would add that once you reach the summit, the most successful people I know bask in the view for a while before heading onto the next mountain to climb.

When I do the same lesson and use the same approach over and over again, I feel like I can predict how it will go. There are few unknowns. But it also means I become stagnant and tend to lose my own curiosity for what may come next. When I am less curious than my students, it comes through loud and clear. On the other hand, when I take risks and step into the unknown *with* my students, we get to cocreate learning together. The psychologist Maslow explained, "You will either step forward into growth, or backward into safety" (Tracy, 2010, p. 35). As teachers, we get to choose this each day.

> When I am less curious than my students, it comes through loud and clear.

What are your areas for growth? What do you need to know and be able to do in order to really live your beliefs?

HOW TO DISCOVER YOUR OWN AREAS FOR GROWTH

We have likely all had the experience of looking for something, getting distracted, and then pausing to realize that we don't even remember what we were looking for. Sometimes I feel like finding our own professional goals and areas of growth can feel foggy. We may know the general area we want to work on further, but the specifics feel elusive. I designed the reflection that follows to help all teachers, no matter their experience level, to drill down on and find clarity with their own areas of growth.

Know Your Strengths

Whenever we create goals for ourselves and seek growth, I suggest we start with strengths. Actually, I use the same process with students, building from what they already know and can do. This creates a solid foundation for us all to learn, no matter the age. Begin by listing your strengths, and then as soon as you get stuck, ask others to help you. You may want to reread feedback from formal evaluations, reread notes from colleagues and students, and when you are feeling brave enough, directly ask your colleagues and mentors, "What do you think my strengths are as a teacher?"

I recently helped a grade-level team do this together during a planning meeting, and it was quite a powerful experience to witness teachers naming each other's strengths. I heard them say, "You are the queen of read-alouds. Your students hang on your every word." And another teacher explained, "You are so organized and deliberate about how you use class time." A third teacher offered, "Your students are able to be themselves around you because you are so real and warm and nurturing." Every teacher beamed, and some turned red (it can be challenging to accept a compliment). I asked each teacher to write the strength down and to hold on to it so we could leverage it when we set our professional goals.

Ask your colleagues for input, and then list your strengths here.

Acknowledge Your Challenges

Once you know and name your strengths, it can be helpful to also acknowledge your challenges. Notice these are not your faults or deficits. Please do not go into judgment mode with yourself. We all have challenges, and these are actually really helpful opportunities to identify our areas of growth. I think of a challenge as having the following characteristics:

- They keep you up at night.

- They propel you forward into wanting to learn more.

- You find yourself talking about them with friends and colleagues.

- You feel a bit stuck or confused.

- You have not faced them before.

- You have more questions than answers around the issue.

- You may feel some resistance to it, knowing you will be stretched.

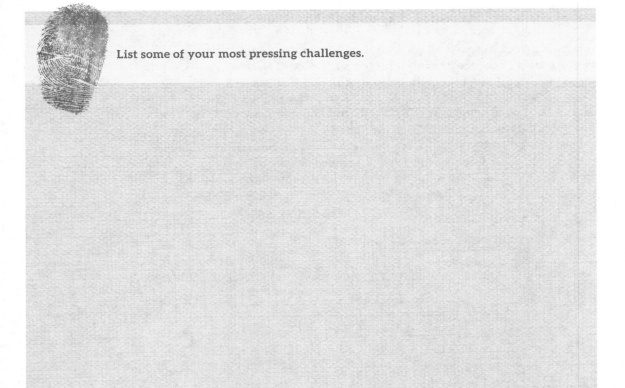

List some of your most pressing challenges.

Some of these characteristics might sound contradictory, and the truth is for me that when I am facing a challenge I often do feel conflicted. Some challenges I feel prepared to face and help me grow my excitement, while other challenges make me want to run in the other direction. Once you write down the challenges, you can sort them into "challenges I cannot wait to tackle" and "challenges I am honestly afraid of." This sorting helps you make different action plans depending on how you are feeling.

Challenges I Cannot Wait to Tackle:	Challenges I Am Honestly Afraid of:

Find Your Unexplored Territories

So you have named strengths and challenges, and the next step is to go explore the territories you have never visited. What I mean by *territory* is an aspect of your teaching practice that you rarely, if ever, explore. What conversations do you avoid? What parts of your teaching do you ignore? These may also be blind spots for you because the very fact that you have not explored them means you might not even know they are there. Use the following reflection chart to begin to reflect on which aspects of your teaching have gotten little to no attention from you. Rate each territory from a zero to three: zero meaning you gave it no attention at all, and three meaning it takes up a lot of your time and energy and focus. Use this reflection on your own or with a learning partner, mentor, or coach.

Territory	How Much Have I Explored This? (0–3)	Reflections
Student independence and transfer		
Student engagement		
Classroom environment		
Planning		
Student collaboration		
Student risk-taking		
Content knowledge		
Assessment		
Other		

Create Your Own Professional Learning Goals

Now that you have reflected on your strengths, challenges, and unexplored territories, reread what you wrote, and list a few possible goals for yourself. You may generate these goals from your strengths. Consider, "How can I leverage this strength even more than I do right now?" One example could be the teacher who is really strong with chapter book read-alouds might consider setting a goal to use read-alouds more in other content areas. You can also set goals from your challenges. For the ones you are excited about, consider turning the challenge into a goal. For example, if you have a challenge with student motivation in math, you can set a goal to learn more ways to help students be self-motivated by learning new teaching practices that tap into intrinsic motivation. For those challenges that scare you, consider finding a mentor or coach to cocreate a goal and help support you on the journey. I will explain more about using coaches and mentors in a few pages. Finally, use your unexplored territories to set goals. Turn the territories where you rarely give your attention into a goal for yourself. For example, if you ranked classroom environment low on your exploration scale, set a goal to study more about flexible seating and how to make the most of the classroom space.

How to Discover Your Own Areas for Growth

★ Know your strengths.

★ Acknowledge your challenges.

★ Find your unexplored territories.

★ Create your own professional learning goals.

What are a few of your current professional learning goals?

HOW TO DESIGN YOUR OWN PROFESSIONAL LEARNING PLANS

When we are in the driver's seat of our professional learning, we get to make the choices. What do we want to study? How do we want to study it? When do we want to study it? Who do we want to collaborate and study with? All of these questions help us make choices about how to use our valuable learning time. I reached out to many teachers and asked them to name their top three ways of driving their professional growth and was struck by how similar their lists were. When I examined this list, I noticed how often professional growth meant broadening our current vision of what is possible and how often it involved other educators. Over and over again, teachers responded by saying they do the following:

- Collaborate with colleagues and coaches.

- Read professional texts.

- Listen to podcasts and attend webinars.

- Attend conferences and workshops.

- Reach out to their professional learning networks (PLNs).

- Ask for feedback from others.

- Visit other classrooms.

- Take risks and reflect on their practice.

Let's first notice just how many of these options are free or very low cost and how many of them are "on the fly" versus preplanned. We teachers are incredibly savvy at finding ways to propel our growth even with a zero-dollar budget. The few options that do cost money often are funded by districts or grants or offer discounts to teachers. In the next sections, I will take us deeper into some of these ways to drive professional growth, offering examples of how to make the most of each option. Based on the list of ways to grow, I divided them up into two main areas: (1) learning with insiders in our schools and (2) learning with outsiders to broaden our perspectives.

LEARN WITH INSIDERS

So your school doesn't have money for substitute teachers and you have obligations that keep you from going to outside workshops; there is no need to stall in your learning. There are so many ways to make the most of growth opportunities right in your building for free. First, you can seek out a learning partner to grow with. Second, take advantage of coaches and mentors in your district or school who are there to support your next steps. Third, remember that your students can offer you the most effective and immediate feedback because they are in your classroom every single day. The only thing that these three in-school approaches require is a willingness to learn something new.

Besides being accessible and free, in-house professional learning leads to huge amounts of growth. According to a 2002 study conducted by Joyce and Showers, presentation of theory and modeling offer only a 5 to 10 percent likelihood of new learning being applied to classroom practices. Peer visitation and coaching, on the other hand, have an 85 to 90 percent likelihood of new learning leading to classroom application. So if you are serious about driving real growth, make sure to incorporate some peer visitation and coaching into your plans.

Learning Partners

One of the most powerful ways to grow as a teacher is to seek out a learning partner. I have had several over the years, but Malini comes to my mind first. Malini and I taught third grade down the hall from each other and were both newcomers to that grade. Malini had years of experience teaching science, and I was still early on in my career. Our collaboration started as totally unplanned meetings and reflection sessions over lunch and hallway conversations. We hosted classroom library parties where we would help each other level and organize our libraries. We'd order in pizza for dinner and stay late into the night, having so much fun getting to know each other and new books.

Then our collaboration became much more intentional. We set up a system to observe each other teaching and sometimes combined our classes and co-taught lessons together. Many of the teaching tips I picked up and still use today, I learned from Malini. She modeled thoughtful and responsive teaching along with holding high expectations for her students. I would plan with her and think, "Third graders can't do this." Then I would go sit in on her class and watch as she did, in fact, set up structures and supports that allowed her students to meet and exceed the goals. More than once, she taught me the power of modeling, having patience, and assuming the best about each student. My collaboration with Malini did not feel like one more thing to get done and instead filled me up and freed up my time because I was more confident and prepared as a teacher.

A learning partner offers you a sounding board, confirms your good ideas, challenges your thinking, and holds you accountable to follow through with plans. No matter what you call them, every teacher benefits from having one (see Chapter 4 for research on relationships). If you haven't found that partner for yourself, then seek out a "matchmaker" who can help you find your Malini. As a literacy coach, I would find myself saying to a teacher, "Do you know so and so? I think the two of you would really collaborate well."

> According to a 2002 study conducted by Joyce and Showers, presentation of theory and modeling offer only a 5 to 10 percent likelihood of new learning being applied to classroom practices.

A learning partner offers you a sounding board, confirms your good ideas, challenges your thinking, and holds you accountable to follow through with plans.

Experienced leaders and mentors who know many teachers can often help you find a learning partner, even if they are not in your school or grade level. Years ago, I played teacher matchmaker when I met Laura and Pam. These two teachers did not teach in the same school or at the same grade level, but I just knew they needed to meet. I approached each of them separately and explained just how amazing the other was. I suggested they meet up and e-mailed them to make the connection. I can now take credit for their friendship and outstanding professional collaboration. They began to use Skype between their classes and went on to co-write blog posts and co-lead after-school courses; now, they both work with me as literacy consultants and teammates. The takeaway here? If you don't know how to find a learning partner who is going to push you and honor your work right in your school, then ask someone to set you up with some possibilities.

Classroom Coaching and Mentoring

If you are fortunate enough to have an instructional coach or mentor in your building, you have an opportunity to take advantage of personalized professional learning. A coach or mentor is someone who will listen and help you set goals, plan with you for how to reach your goals, model lessons to deepen your practice, and offer you feedback for what is working and what else you might try with your students.

While many teachers are fearful that a coach is there to "fix" something wrong in their classroom and shy away from the opportunity, this couldn't be further from the truth. Think about the fact that most elite and already accomplished athletes have coaches and mentors. Coaching expert Jim Knight (2007) explains, "Coaches are nonevaluative and respect teachers' professionalism and focus their efforts on conversations that lead to creative, practical application of best practices."

Seek out your school's coach or your mentor, and set up a time to meet. She may have ideas for how to get started, and you may want to follow her lead. Or you may want to be proactive and explicitly tell the coach what you want to focus on. In fact, this book is meant to serve as a self-coaching platform, so you may want to use some of the practices and ideas in here to begin choosing a focus. If you want to just watch your coach teach all of the time, challenge yourself to do some of the teaching so you can also reap the benefits of nonevaluative feedback. I tend to follow the gradual release of responsibility model in coaching, just as I do with students. First, the coach models. Then, the coach and teacher co-plan and co-teach together. Next, the teacher coaches and the coach jumps in or offers feedback at the end. Trust the coaching process, and know that everyone who offers you feedback can help you on your quest for professional growth.

Student Feedback

In addition to finding a learning partner and taking advantage of classroom coaching, it can be really helpful to elicit feedback from students as a driver of professional growth. It always bugged me that college students are often the only ones who are asked to fill out evaluations for their professors and that the information is collected after the course is already over. As a professor, I would eagerly await the evaluation feedback and oftentimes wished I had been given the feedback much earlier so I could have made adjustments during the course. So . . . this is what I began doing. I created a brief digital reflection for students to fill out after every course meeting session. While it was optional, students knew that I would take their comments and use them to adjust the next week's course plans. I found out which articles students liked and found beneficial and which ones they didn't enjoy. I found out when they felt stressed and wanted more time and when they wanted to go back and review a concept from a previous session. I also found out what they found most helpful and wanted more of. So much of teaching can feel like we are walking in the dark. Simply asking our students how it is going and what else they need shines a light on our next step.

While K–12 teachers cannot possibly ask for formal feedback after every class, we can periodically set aside time to hear students' perspectives. One way to get student feedback is to ask them to fill out a formal feedback form. You can choose to make this anonymous or personal. Use your values and goals to create questions or keep it simple and consistent. A few sample questions include the following:

- What has been most helpful for you so far in this course or unit?

- What do you want more of?

- What has been the biggest challenge for you so far in this course or unit?

- What do you want less of?

- How can I help you to reach your goals?

- What else do you want me to consider when planning the rest of the course or unit?

Another way to get feedback from students is to have reflective conversations with them. You can do this one on one, in small groups, or as a whole class. You might ask the same questions you would have asked in writing, or you may keep it more casual and conversational. So many students will appreciate the time you are taking to hear their reflections, and you are modeling how to listen openly.

A third way to get feedback from students is to look at their daily engagement and learning. Not all students can and will articulate their reflections about your teaching, but all students can show you what they do and don't want to do and what they can and cannot yet do. When you begin to view each class experience as a form of feedback, you can notice patterns and trends. In what sorts of lessons do students really engage? Which lessons get bored and blank stares? When students seem confused or unwilling to take risks, view it as feedback for you. What else might you try or how else might you frame this lesson?

When we take the time to elicit feedback from students, they let us know where we need to grow and move next. Here is just one example. An honors chemistry teacher I worked with asked her students to fill out a form about what was and was not working for them in her class. This alone made her a super brave and open teacher. She found out that all of her students mentioned the textbook in some negative way. They said it was too dull, not clear, and poorly organized, and they hated it. Many admitted they didn't even read it anymore and faked their way through the class assignments. The teacher used this feedback to have a conversation with the class asking for their advice about what to do about this problem. She admitted she was not sure what to use other than the textbook because that is how she learned chemistry herself. At the end of the conversation she said, "Okay. I hear you. I am honestly not sure what other resources we can use to supplement this textbook, but I will make this my goal to find out." She not only created a professional goal of finding more engaging and accessible texts for her students to read but she also showed her students she would be responsive to their needs. This led her to sign up for coaching sessions with me and to learn ways to find more accessible and interesting texts for her students to read.

> So much of teaching can feel like we are walking in the dark. Simply asking our students how it is going and what else they need helps shine a light on our next step.

Seeking Professional Learning Opportunities With Insiders

★ Find a learning partner.

  - Plan and reflect together.
  - Visit each other's classrooms.

★ Say yes to a coach or mentor.

  - Plan for goals together.
  - Co-teach.
  - Get tips and ideas.

★ Ask your students for feedback.

  - Offer written feedback forms.
  - Listen to reflective conversations.
  - Use engagement as a mirror.

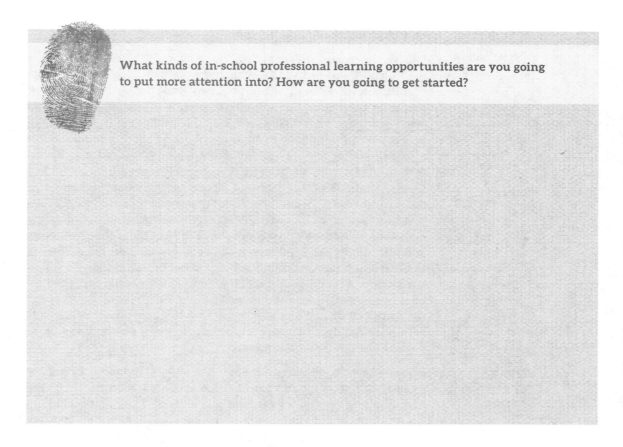

What kinds of in-school professional learning opportunities are you going to put more attention into? How are you going to get started?

LEARN WITH OUTSIDERS

In addition to learning from those who have an insider perspective in your school or district, it can also be beneficial to seek growth opportunities from people who are outside your school. When we spend all of our time narrowly focusing on our local context, we can lose sight of all that is possible in other places that we may want to import into our own classroom. The invention of social media tools has created PLNs that allow teachers from around the world to connect and learn together. Authors who write professional books don't just teach in their books but also blog, lead webinars, and post an abundance of free resources online. Your favorite professional book author is just a tweet or e-mail away, and they thrive on responding to teachers' questions. Many teachers also reflect that some of their most meaningful learning has happened in workshops and conferences they attend and then bring back to their own classrooms. By studying with people who work hundreds or thousands of miles away, we teachers have access to so many ideas that our biggest challenge is often sifting through them all.

Find Your Tribe

English clergyman and poet John Donne famously expressed, "No man is an island/Entire of itself/Every man is a piece of the continent/A part of the main…." Even those of us teachers who consider ourselves most authentic when alone benefit from connecting to "the mainland" or, as Seth Godin says, a tribe. Godin (2014) explains that a tribe is a group of people who are connected to an idea and to one another and who have a shared interest and ways of communicating. While you may have a tribe in your school, many teachers are extending their tribes or finding them in all the corners of the world. Here is just one example. A few years ago, I wrote a book focused on student independence and as a result was invited to participate in several Twitter chats on the topic. I noticed several other educators tended to show up and participate on similar chats and with similar ideas. While it took over a year to meet many of these teachers in person, I felt connected to each one and what we were collectively creating simply by having these "chats" on a regular basis. I ended up presenting with some of these educators at a national conference, and the collaboration was seamless because we had taken the time to really get to know and help each other over the last year online. We are now professional colleagues and friends.

If you are new to finding an online tribe (aka PLN), then I suggest the following to get yourself started. Create a Twitter account. Search for friends or authors you admire, and follow them. Then find a chat and simply watch and like a few tweets you connect to. Next time, actually participate in the chat by adding in your own insights and retweeting tweets you really connect with. If you are not sure how to find a chat, you can reference this curated and updated list of popular education chats: https://sites.google.com/site/twittereducationchats/education-chat-official-list. Twitter is not the only way to connect with a PLN. You can find Facebook groups dedicated to professional books or approaches too. We have a *Teach Like Yourself* Facebook group you may want to pause and join right now at **https://www.facebook.com/groups/teachlikeyourself/**.

Here are some ways to use a PLN:

Be generous.

- Share examples and photos from your classroom.

- Respond to someone else's questions or challenges.

- Retweet or repost when the person is looking for more perspectives.

- Like tweets and posts to show support.

Ask for help.

- Share challenges from your classroom.

- Ask a question, and tag a few people who may be able to help you.

- Let people know what resources you are already using.

- Follow people who may be able to help you. Read what they are posting.

A PLN is not a place to vent, complain, or criticize others. The whole idea of a PLN is a network of professionals who are all seeking to grow in similar areas and can count on each other for helpful support.

Read, Listen, and View Professional Texts

The only way to stay up to date on the latest research and thinking used to be waiting for the journal of your professional organization to come out a few times a year. Now, many researchers and authors publish on a daily, weekly, or monthly basis online and for free. Use your PLN to find and subscribe to some blogs or websites that offer regular support. I know my own team of literacy consultants blog at least once a week, and many of our topics come directly from questions that teachers ask us when we visit their classrooms. Find your author mentors, and most likely they will blog too.

Study professional texts in book clubs. Find a book that is particularly compelling to you or that answers a question that you are trying to figure out. Then find a few learning partners to join in on the nerdy fun. Many authors of professional books also create book study guides you can uses or you can create your own. Meet on a regular basis with your book club, and discuss the ideas in theory but also in regard to what you will actually practice. If you are not sure how to run a professional book club, here is one way it could go:

1. Choose a book.

2. Enlist some learning partners to join you (either in your school or virtually).

3. Make a plan. Schedule the meeting dates and which chapters will be read by each date.

4. Create some norms for the meeting time. How do you want them to go, and what is and is not okay for creating a safe space to share?

5. Read the book. This is obvious, but no one likes it when a book club member shows up without actually doing the reading. If you struggle making time for it, ask your club for tips on how to fit it in.

6. End each meeting with some clear next steps to try out. Hold each other accountable to take the agreed-upon actions, and begin the next session asking people to share how it went.

7. Optional: Reach out to the author. Many authors have websites, Twitter handles, and Facebook pages where you can share your takeaways and ask your questions.

8. Make your learning public. Ask your administrators if your club can share at the next faculty meeting, or write your own blog post summary so that people who were not in your club can learn from you too.

There is a *Teach Like Yourself* book study guide to help facilitate your reading and discussions around this book. You can find it in the appendix.

In addition to reading professional books, there are other ways to seek ideas from experts. Attend webinars, listen to podcasts, and sign up for online courses. You can use a similar framework for book clubs with these other forms of professional texts. View or listen together with colleagues, or meet up with them afterward to discuss next steps you will try out together. Whatever your professional goal, someone is likely writing or talking about it right now. Use your PLN to find that right-in-time resource now.

Attend Workshops, Conferences, and Unconferences

While I already discussed many free or very low-cost ways to drive your professional growth, it is also worthwhile to invest in high-quality workshops and conferences. Your national or regional professional organization offers conferences that often bring in authors, researchers, and teachers to share ideas for its members. Most of these organizations host a conference every year and offer some sort of scholarships or funding for educators. You may also elect to apply to present at a conference and ask your district to help pay for your expenses. The following is a list of some of the largest professional organizations to get you started.

Professional Organizations
• AASL (American Association of School Librarians; www.ala.org/aasl)
• ACTFL (American Council on the Teaching of Foreign Languages; www.actfl.org)
• AECT (Association for Educational Communications and Technology; www.aect.org)
• ASCD (Association for Supervision and Curriculum Development; www.ascd.org)
• ILA (International Literacy Association; www.literacyworldwide.org)
• ISTE (International Society for Technology in Education; www.iste.org)
• NAEA (National Art Education Association; www.arteducators.org)
• NafME (National Association for Music Education; www.nafme.org)
• NAGC (National Association for Gifted Children; www.nagc.org)
• NCSS (National Council for the Social Studies; www.ncss.org)
• NCTE (National Council of Teachers of English; www2.ncte.org)
• NCTM (National Council of Teachers of Mathematics; www.nctm.org)
• NSTA (National Science Teachers Association; www.nsta.org)

In addition to professional organizations, many publishers, authors, and consultants offer local workshops. While it can be challenging to take a day away from your students—this means substitute plans and possibly a bit of a commute—it is often worth it. Say yes when your administrator offers you the opportunity to attend a workshop. In addition, many colleges or professional development organizations offer summer institutes. Summer is a great time to relax and regroup but also a perfect time to take a week for your own professional study. Some of the most rewarding and impactful learning of my career happened at summer institutes because they helped me focus on just my own learning and being a student again for those few days. I began the next school year inspired and ready to begin anew.

Recently, educators have taken professional learning and collaboration into new realms with the advent of unconferences and edcamps. Both of these are teacher-run and all about sharing best practices and innovations. Do a simple search online, and find out when and where your local edcamp will happen. Be prepared to sign up to teach or attend a session right in the moment when you arrive. These experiences are low cost, no frills, and all about teacher-to-teacher collaboration.

Ways to Seek Professional Learning With Outsiders

★ Find your tribe with an online PLN.

- Participate in chats.
- Look for connections.
- Be generous.
- Ask for help.

★ Read, listen, and view professional texts.

- Participate in book clubs.
- Attend webinars.
- Tune into podcasts.

★ Attend workshops, conferences, and unconferences.

- Join professional organizations.
- Learn at conferences.
- Join an unconference or edcamp.

CONNECT PROFESSIONAL LEARNING TO BELIEFS AND GOALS

With so many possibilities for professional learning, it can be challenging to focus and not get overwhelmed. It is unlikely that you can participate in every Twitter chat or read every professional book. Go back to the goals you set earlier in this chapter, and use them to help you choose how and where you will begin your study. Without a connection to your larger purpose and practices, online resources can become shiny toys that distract us from what we think really matters.

If you have been using the reflection spaces in this book, it is a good time to go back and reread all of your writing so far. Notice patterns and trends. Star or highlight the insights and ideas that you feel most energized about. Now use those starred parts to streamline and focus on your professional learning plan, possibly revising what you already wrote down to become even more crystal clear. Just like you make plans for your students, your own learning and growth are worth your time and attention. You might even want to show this plan to your instructional coach, mentor, learning partner, or supervisor so they can help support you.

I feel the need to give a bit of caution here too. While there are many online resources at your fingertips, be careful to seek out research-based and reliable ones to actually study. Websites like Pinterest and Teachers Pay Teachers often are full of color and cuteness but short on substance. Or worse, many of those pinned posts are stolen content from an author's work. It is worth the time to seek out the original author's work and to make sure there is some research and validity behind those tips you found. Remember that no matter where you study, start with your why, and make sure it aligns with your vision and practices. As we end this chapter, take some time to work on your own professional learning plan and put yourself firmly in the driver's seat.

Make a professional learning plan for yourself.

My Professional Goals	How I Will Work Toward My Goals

TAKE
CARE OF YOURSELF

Video 6

Source: One 21 Production

An empty lantern provides no light. Self-care is the fuel that allows it to shine vibrantly, lighting the way for others.

—Project Happiness @projecthappiness

As a new teacher, I jumped headfirst into every opportunity that came my way. When a new school committee needed another member, I raised my hand. When a friend needed help packing and moving, I showed up with packing tape. When local college students needed a classroom to do some research in, I e-mailed a positive reply. I actually was interested in joining and saying yes to many of the opportunities that arrived at my door, but there was often a breaking point when I just couldn't imagine fitting in one more thing. I let my fear of disappointing others cloud my judgment of just how much I could actually handle. I was afraid that saying no to one opportunity meant I would not get tenure, I would lose a friend, or I would miss a chance to grow. When I look back now, I guess I had FOMO (fear of missing out) before I even knew that was a real thing.

The cost of saying yes to everything was my own sense of well-being. My energy sapped, I began to resent the people and organizations I had said yes to. It culminated in a serious health issue when I contracted pneumonia during my fourth year of teaching. I was so sick I couldn't get out of bed. My temperature soared. Fluid filled my lungs. I missed almost two weeks of teaching. This was a big sign that I needed to cut back on all I signed up to do. Can you relate?

I didn't fully understand what was really going on until years later, when I happened upon a podcast where I heard the author Byron Katie speak about "honest nos." She was being interviewed by Oprah, and she explained that when we say yes to people when we know we don't have any more to give, we are being dishonest. She went on to coach Oprah to consider the importance of an honest no—one where you are turning down an option because it just doesn't feel right or you just don't have enough time and energy to really commit. While listening to this interview, I gasped and felt the tension release in my shoulders and neck. That weight of saying yes was something I had been carrying on my back for years.

The idea of honest yeses and honest nos made me realize I needed to listen to myself, more than I needed to listen to the fear of missing out or disappointing someone else. I worried this was a selfish act until I began to actually take care of myself and realize that I was a much better and more energized teacher and person when I was well. We all know the line we hear when flying: "Put your oxygen mask on first before assisting others." The reason behind this is that we cannot help others when we ourselves are struggling to survive. So it is actually not selfish to prioritize your own well-being when it also has a big impact on your ability to help others.

If I am really honest, I still struggle with taking care of myself and practicing honest nos. It seems like every year or two I need another reminder, which usually turns up as a health-related issue to wake me up from the fog of busyness. So as I write this chapter, it is for all of you teachers who could benefit from prioritizing self-care, and it is also for me. I need to read my own words and remember to put them into action myself.

CREATE SPACE FOR YOURSELF

When I first heard the term *self-care*, I rolled my eyes. My yoga teacher used her soft, calm voice to explain what it was while I lay in *savasana* at the end of a yoga class. Okay, I may not have rolled my eyes because they were shut, but I was doing it on the inside. "Did this woman have any idea how busy I was? Didn't she understand that this yoga class itself was a challenge for me to fit in my schedule?" I thought. I actually became agitated the more I thought about self-care and left the class worked up instead of relaxed and renewed. Over the years, I recognized my own triggered reactions as a sign that I needed to pay more attention to something. Since this concept got me so worked up, there must be something that I needed to consider.

I spent that weekend after the yoga class making a list of all I needed to get done in the following week. The list was prioritized by obligation and then color coded by category. In the past, my list-making had always made me feel calmer and more prepared for the week ahead. But something was off this time. I began to obsessively think about the list. Then I grudgingly added a few more items to the list based on the advice of my yoga teachers. I added in spaces for rest and unscheduled time to feel out what I needed in that moment. I just wasn't sure where I would fit this free time. Then, during my weekend-long training run, I listened to a podcast with Eckhart Tolle. He explained how we could each find time every single day for quiet space if we simply approached it one breath at a time. For example, he said that when the phone rings, take a long, slow, intentional breath before answering it. A single breath can be a meditation if we approach it with that purpose in mind. I decided even busy me could find the time and space for single breaths of calmness. As I began to find these small moments of space, I felt myself relax and my anxiety slip away. I imagined my shoulders releasing tension and my exhalation letting go of all the stuff that was cluttering my mind. How much space do you give yourself in any given day?

Find Small Moments in Your Day

While there is no prescription for how to find space in your day, I encourage you to seek it out and find it in all the small spaces it may be hiding. Here are some questions and actions you may take to locate your "me-time moments." As you reflect on the following questions, try not

> A single breath can be a meditation if we approach it with that purpose in mind.

to judge yourself or make excuses for why you can't find more space. That sort of self-talk leaves us feeling even more stressed and depleted. Recall back in Chapter 3 that when we prime ourselves for personal power, we can accomplish much more than viewing ourselves or our situations as powerless. You do have the power to find some space for yourself and can start with just one breath at a time.

- Are there times of the day you find yourself zoning out on social media? What would it be like to take back that time for yourself? How might you spend it instead?

- How do you spend your waiting time (at the grocery store, at school pickup time, while waiting for your takeout, etc.)? How might you make the most of this time for some calm and purposeful relaxation?

- Notice your morning routine. While you may savor every last minute in bed, what would it be like to wake up five minutes earlier and not rush? How might you spend those five minutes on yourself? How do you want to purposefully start your day?

- How do you end your day? Do you check e-mails one more time before bed? Fall asleep in front of the television? How might you create a calming and unwinding routine before bed?

- How often do you check your e-mail and phone? Can you set some parameters and "no phones" time where you unplug from others for even a few minutes a day?

Create Boundaries

In his book *Deep Work: Rules for Focused Success in a Distracted World*, author Cal Newport (2016) explains why it is essential to set boundaries that allow us to do deep work. Deep work allows us to stay focused on the learning at hand and to gain new insights by paying attention to just one thing at a time. One study he cites was conducted by Tom Cochran (2013), the chief technology officer at a large media company. He decided to study and quantify how much time and money was spent on e-mails in his company. He found that on average he received 511 e-mail messages a week and sent 284 messages. Even if he spent only thirty seconds per e-mail, it cost him an hour and a half per day moving information around. When he calculated this by the number of employees who were also e-mailing, he found that the company spent over a million dollars a year on processing e-mails. One step further, he found that each e-mail cost about ninety-five cents to process. There was no way the cost matched the results. This study and others led businesses to set clear boundaries on the amount of time spent on e-mails and social media. One successful consulting company decided to have each consultant take one day off per week from sending or reading messages. While it was at first a nerve-racking experiment, they found that it led to more productivity and a stronger sense of well-being (Newport, 2016, p. 58). As teachers, we can take a tip from businesses and allow ourselves to set some boundaries so we can do deep work while at school and develop a balanced and less stressful life when we leave for the day.

One way to figure out the boundaries we want to set is to use a calendar. We likely all have some sort of digital calendar on our smartphones these days, and we plug in our events, appointments, reminders, and alerts. For me, I keep the calendar on my phone so I don't forget the tenth errand I need to run or the deadline for the project I signed up for. My calendar doesn't include everything I do each day, especially not the repeating, daily stuff that fills my days. I don't include "make dinner" or "do laundry" or "write lesson plans" on my phone's calendar. I think I exclude these tasks because they are going to get done even without the alert on my phone. But when I don't include them, I am getting a very false picture of how I spend my time.

I recently decided to go "old school" and write out my weekly schedule and tasks on a paper planner for a few weeks and see what I found. I wrote out all the main events such as make lunches for the week, do laundry, return e-mails, call my mom, etc. Since they didn't all fit in the space provided by the company that made the planners, I ended up writing in teeny-tiny print. At the end of each day, I went back to the planner and checked off what I did, I crossed out what I didn't do, and I moved things that didn't get done but still needed to be completed at some point that week. This process led me to the bullet journal phenomenon that has gone viral.

Bullet journals are a system created by Ryder Carroll with the following tagline: "Where productivity meets mindfulness" (http://bulletjournal .com/blog). The mindfulness piece of the bullet journal is what intrigued me most. To make the most of the system, you can reflect on how you spend your time, set priorities, and carve out time rather than impulsively do something the second it pops into your mind. It helped me set some boundaries based on my priority for more time and space.

Here is just one example of how I mindfully created a boundary. I have the Twitter app on my phone that allows me to know when I am tagged or mentioned in a tweet or when one of my tweets gets some retweets. This means as long as I am looking at my phone or have the sound turned on, I would impulsively check the app every time I heard the ding of the alert. I listed "participate with my PLN on Twitter" in my bullet journal. Then I decided to carve out time for when I could actually participate and not feel obligated to be tethered to my phone all day, every day. I set a boundary by deciding when in the day I would and would not check my Twitter account. I took the sound alert off my phone, and this new-found freedom allowed me to have a little more space in the day.

Take a moment to think about the boundaries you might want to create for yourself so you can actually have a few minutes back each day for yourself. The following are ideas that teachers have shared with me that might work for you too.

- *Physical boundary example:* Park your car as far as possible, and leave your lunch or snack in the car (weather permitting). At lunchtime, you can take a purposeful stroll to get your food and use that time to relax and take in the fresh air.

- *Communication boundary example:* Set an auto response on your e-mail during the weekend that says you will respond to e-mails during the week. Let people know you are unplugging over the weekend so you don't feel pressure to respond on a Sunday night.

- *Activities example:* After looking at your detailed calendar, notice how much time you really have for activities, and set a boundary about how many you will say yes to. For example, you may decide on only two activities that week. Once you say yes to two things, simply say no to the others so you don't overcommit.

Make the Most of Mornings or Me-Time Evenings

Almost everyone I speak to says they are not a morning person, including the person I wake up next to every day. Laura Vanderkam (2012), author of *What the Most Successful People Do Before Breakfast*, claims that the morning time, before work begins, is the best time to nurture yourself. Her research is full of examples of successful and happy people who use their mornings to exercise, pray, meditate, read, or write. They choose the experiences that bring them joy and well-being and do them first thing in the day so they actually get done. As the day goes on and the demands of others pile up, it becomes an act of willpower to actually do the self-nurturing behaviors that you crave, and they often get pushed aside due to fatigue or other commitments. Vanderkam offers five steps for making the most of your mornings so they can be the most impactful of your day.

1. *Track your time:* For at least a week, keep track of how you use your time—and not just the morning times—so you can better understand how you use it.

2. *Picture the perfect morning:* Spend time visualizing what your perfect morning would look like, and sketch, describe, or list what you see.

3. *Think through the logistics:* Make this ideal morning a ritual, and make a plan for how long you will spend on each part and what you need to make it happen.

4. *Build the habit:* Habits take time to become strong, so you may need to really motivate yourself at first. Positive psychologist Shawn Achor (2010) recommends thinking about what you are grateful for and looking forward to as you wake up and think about your day because what your brain focuses on becomes your reality (p. 31).

5. *Tune up as necessary:* Be flexible with your routines, and allow yourself the ability to change or revise your plans as needed.

Vanderkam (2012) explains, "When you make over your mornings, you can make over your life" (p. 33). There have been years of my life when I ran with my running group at 5:30 a.m. Getting out of bed was always painful, but the resulting energy surge and boost was so worth it. Other times in my life I chose to begin my day with fifteen minutes of meditation before jumping in the shower or making my tea. I don't know anyone who ever regrets getting started with some sort of self-care routine. The hardest part is just getting started.

If you are a night owl, apply these five strategies to enhance the quality of your evening hours. I have friends who write, paint, or compose music best at night—perhaps after the family is asleep and they have the quiet time they need. They have developed deeply satisfying habits that allow them to "wind down" and recharge for the next day productively.

Breathe Intentionally

Day or night, another way to create more space for yourself is to breathe deeply with intention. When my mind won't cooperate with me telling it to relax, I rely on changing my breathing. While I first learned about slowing down breathing in my yoga teacher training class, I then read more about it from medical doctors and researchers. Consciously choosing to breathe differently is not just a yoga practice; it is a research-proven tool to regulate our nervous system. In basic terms, when our brain perceives something as threatening (such as making a lesson very high stakes), it activates our amygdala, which then sends us into fight, flight, or freeze mode. This is called the sympathetic nervous system. When this gets triggered, we literally cannot access other parts of our brain such as our memory (there goes priming) and higher-level thinking. The only thing we can do to shift our nervous system response is to calm our brain and body.

The easiest way to slow our breathing is to breathe more fully from our belly up through our lungs and in through our nostrils. Then we can exhale slowly through our noses and try to extend the exhalation longer than the inhalation. This triggers us into the parasympathetic nervous system response often described as rest and relaxation. By practicing this calm and slow breathing, we can regain our full brain's function and begin priming ourselves for feeling like powerful teachers.

Create Space for Yourself
★ Find small moments in your day.
★ Create boundaries.
★ Make the most of mornings or me-time evenings.
★ Breathe intentionally.

For those of you who like the idea of having more personal space but then feel a bit doubtful you can pull it off or you wonder if you really deserve it, take a few minutes to reflect on what it feels like to not have any space for yourself and what it feels like to have some moments of space. Jot down your observations so you can come back to this description, and remind yourself why it is vital that you make space a priority.

What does it feel like when I have no space for myself at all?	What does it feel like when I have some space for myself?

FOCUS ON HAPPINESS

When we are happy, we are better and more successful at our work (Achor, 2010). This means that our personal happiness is not a luxury or an added bonus; it is an essential part of being an effective teacher. This doesn't mean we hide or suppress the many other feelings that come up for us, but it does mean that being happy in our overall lives is vital.

Pay Attention to Your Frame

Our ability to frame our life experiences in the most generous and positive way is a key aspect of being happy. In their book *The Book of Joy*, the Dalai Lama, Desmond Tutu, and Douglas Abrams (2016) help us understand how our outlook and thoughts shape our ability to experience joy:

> A healthy perspective really is the foundation of joy and happiness, because the way we see the world is the way we experience the world. Changing the way we see the world in turn changes the way we feel and the way we act, which changes the world itself... with our mind we create our own world. (p. 194)

Abrams goes on to quote Viktor E. Frankl (1959), whose book *Man's Search for Meaning* illustrates how our perspective toward life is our ultimate human freedom (Dalai Lama et al., 2016).

While their book shares many ways to live a more joyful life, a few that struck me most do center around the concept that our perspective affects our sense of joy. They explain that people who take a wider perspective than their own personal vantage point are more joyful. They cite several studies that show that "being too self-regarding really does make us unhappy" (Dalai Lama et al., 2016, p. 200). One study found an association between people who use more personal pronouns and increased risk of heart attacks. Another study suggested that people's degree of "self-involvement" may be a better predictor of death than smoking, cholesterol levels, and high blood pressure. A third study found that people who often use first-person singular pronouns (*I, me*) are more likely to be depressed than people who use first-person plural pronouns (*we, us*). What all three of these studies reveal is that when we focus our perspective too much on ourselves and our own struggles, our health, happiness, and well-being decline.

So how does this research on being too self-regarding connect to taking care of yourself? On the surface, it may seem like this is contradictory, but in fact, it is actually interrelated. In order for us to be happy, we need to take care of ourselves by creating space for nurturing our own needs, *and* we also benefit from viewing our life experiences from the broadest perspective that allows us to see other people's experiences along with our own. Taking care of ourselves does not mean we disregard others; it means we step back so we can actually get the perspective that allows us to see the largest possible picture. When we take this wider perspective, we are more grateful for our life experiences and relationships.

Let's take it a step further and really connect these ideas.

When we focus our perspective too much on ourselves and our own struggles, our health, happiness, and well-being decline.

Be a Contribution

When we do finally carve out some moments for ourselves, it is important to consider where our mind goes and the ways we frame our reflections. Authors Benjamin and Rosamund Zander (2002) draw a distinction between focusing on success and failure versus focusing on contribution. They claim that when we are driven to be successful and avoid failure, we end up suffering due to the anxiety and pressure this produces. On the other hand, they suggest we focus on how much we have contributed each day. In other words, consider how you can be of service to others. They explain, "In the game of contribution you wake up each day and bask in the notion that you are a gift to others" (Zander & Zander, 2002, p. 58). They point out there is no negative flip side to being a contribution, unlike being successful, whose flip side is being a failure. They beautifully share this:

> Naming oneself and others as a contribution produces a shift away from self-concern and engages us in a relationship with others that is an arena for making a difference. Rewards in the contribution game are of a deep and enduring kind, though less predictable than the trio of money, fame, and power that accrue to the winner in the success game. You never know what they will be, or from whence they will come. (p. 63)

One way to avoid the pitfalls of turning our self-nurturing and reflection time into a self-regarding time that leads to unhappiness is to focus on how you have contributed to others and how they have contributed to you. This is a form of gratitude practice that leads to a profound sense of purpose and joy. So there really is no contradiction between carving out time for yourself and being too self-focused because it all depends on how you frame that time. In order to avoid the self-regarding that is dangerous, use self-care as a form of rejuvenation. You can be of service to others, viewing your work and your self-care as an act of kindness to others, knowing you need to be healthy and happy to do that well.

One example that comes to my mind is the way young-adult author Jason Reynolds measures his success, not just by book sales or awards but by how he is positively affecting youth. In his interview on *The Daily Show*, he explains how he writes books for kids like he was so that they see their lives as having value and worthy of being the subjects of books. He is driven by writing authentic tales, and he views his role as being a contribution. All of the hours he spends alone, dreaming up stories, and then writing them down, he explains, are a privilege. He said, "I am of service to young people. They are not of service to me. I am grateful that they allow me the space to honor them with my stories. These are love notes" (Reynolds, 2018). What a powerful example Reynolds models for us about how to be a contribution.

Believe in Possibility

In addition to writing about being a contribution, Zander and Zander (2002) write about the power of possibility: "The more attention you shine on a particular subject, the more evidence it will grow. Attention is like light and air and water. Shine attention on obstacles and problems and they multiply lavishly" (p. 108). If, on the other hand, you shine attention on what is possible, you begin to see evidence of all that possibility growing.

One of the ways we can focus on possibility is a practice called enrollment. Enrollment is "the art and practice of generating a spark of possibility for others to share.... Enrollment is about giving yourself as a possibility to others and being ready, in turn, to catch their spark" (Zander & Zander, 2002, pp. 125–126). I just love this idea of thinking about possibility as a spark that we can offer others. I see this playing out each and every day I work with young children. Just one example is the way I see kindergarten students gaining enrollment from each other during partner reading time. I recently watched as two five-year-old girls put their books down next to each other. The first girl asked her partner, "What was your book about?" As the second girl began to answer, she interrupted and prompted, "You need to show me the pages of the book so I can see too." Then she leaned closer and began pointing at pictures with her partner. Both readers sat side by side, engrossed in the book, and shared a spark of reading energy. At the end of the conversation, the first girl said, "Now let's switch books so we can read each other's." I could feel their excited energy and see the joy that enrolling each other in reading brought.

As adults, it can be difficult to share these sparks. We might be worried or self-conscious. It is cool to be super excited about learning when you are five years old. At thirty-five years old, it can often feel much less cool to be so obviously excited. In my experience, when we don't share the spark of our own excitement we can't enroll others in joining us. Luckily, Zander and Zander (2002) offer four steps for gaining enrollment from others:

1. Imagine that people are an invitation for enrollment. Act as if they want to join you or for you to join them.

2. Stand ready to participate, willing to be moved and inspired.

3. Offer that which lights you up.

4. Have no doubt that others are eager to catch the spark.

These four steps can be taken with anyone you want to connect with and enroll in your joy journey. Maybe it is a friend? A partner? A colleague? A family member? Be the kind of person who looks for opportunities for enrollment, and notice how much happier you become.

Be the kind of person who looks for opportunities for enrollment, and notice how much happier you become.

Don't Take Yourself Too Seriously

One of my all-time favorite stories is also from Zander and Zander's (2002) book (can you tell I love this book?). In this story, there are two prime ministers from different states. All of a sudden a man bursts into their room and begins shouting and banging his fists on the table. The hosting prime minister kindly tells the irate man, "Remember rule number six." The man calms down and apologizes and leaves the room. A little while later, a woman comes in and begins anxiously speaking and moving around the room. Again, the hosting prime minister calmly states, "Please remember rule six." She also apologizes and steps out of the room. When they are interrupted a third time and again the prime minister suggests the person remember rule number six, the visiting prime minister asks, "I have to know, what is rule number six?" The host smiles and says, "Rule number six is *don't take yourself so seriously*." The visitor pauses to let this soak in and asks, "What are the other rules?" The host smiles and says, "We don't have any other rules. We don't need them."

I have read this story dozens of times because it is just so perfect. If we remember rule number six, so many other issues just fade away. The ability to lighten up is a gift to ourselves and all of those around us. It helps us remember that humor is one of the best ways to get over ourselves. Whenever you find yourself in the grips of losing your cool, getting tangled up in drama, or beating yourself up, stop and remind yourself of rule number six.

Make sure you find something to laugh about every day. Research from embodied cognition reveals that our bodies affect our learning, thinking, and feeling. One study showed that Botox injections into patients' faces had a dramatic impact on combating depression because people literally could not frown. Another study found that people were less likely to find a story funny when they held a pencil between pursed lips. Many studies have found that people who attend laughter clubs—places where people purposefully come together to laugh—have higher levels of happiness (Beilock, 2015). What all three of these findings show is that how we hold our bodies affects our levels of happiness. It can help to laugh every day, to smile more, and to be aware of how you are carrying yourself. These subtle body cues send messages to your brain to experience certain kinds of feelings. Watching a funny show or finding a local improv or comedy club are all forms of self-care because the effects of laughter lead to spikes in joy and well-being.

The Dalai Lama clearly explains the connection between laughter and well-being. He explains, "It is much better when there is not too much seriousness. Laughter, joking is much better. Then we can be completely relaxed … it is very good for your heart and health in general" (Dalai Lama et al., 2016, p. 216). The Archbishop Desmond Tutu elaborates on the positive role of humor by explaining, "I don't think I woke up and presto I am funny. I think it is something you can cultivate. Like anything else, it is a skill.… Start looking for the humor in life, and you will find it. You will stop asking, why me? And start recognizing that life happens to all of us" (p. 222). While humor is such a personalized and nuanced element, one commonality is that we all need it to be happy. Look for and seek out more opportunities to laugh, and see how much it changes your outlook and perspective.

Take these dispositions to work every day. Teaching like yourself means being yourself in the classroom. If being witty makes you feel happy, let students see that side of you. If you need to retreat for a few minutes to unwind or recharge, have the class pull out their independent books and grab that quiet time, sip that mug of tea—whatever it is you need. One teacher I know has set up this morning routine with her fifth graders so that she knows she's got this breathing room once a day. She taught the students to come in quietly while she has calming music in the background. The students put their bags and belongings away and then pull out their writing notebooks, taking about five minutes to read or write as a centering activity before the teaching day begins. When I taught third grade, I often needed a minute or two before each lesson to feel prepared. I taught my students how to give me that space with a daily routine. One student's job was to ring a set of chimes I had hanging up. As the chimes rang, the students gathered the materials they would need, pushed in their chairs, and silently walked over to the class rug where we met for daily lessons. They sat down in an assigned seat and waited for me to begin teaching. Once they learned how to do this routine, it ran smoothly without me needing to do anything. It helped students come to the lesson focused and calm, and it gave me an extra minute to come prepared to teach.

Focus on Happiness

★ Pay attention to your frame.

★ Be a contribution.

★ Believe in possibility.

★ Don't take yourself too seriously.

What makes you happy? How might you make more time for what brings you joy?

HELP YOUR STUDENTS TAKE CARE OF THEMSELVES

Once we learn to take good care of ourselves, to nurture ourselves, to carve out time, and to cultivate our own happiness, we can model this for our students. By simply being a happy person, you will be a more joyful teacher too. I had this science teacher when I was a middle school student who seemed so incredibly happy and excited to learn each day that I couldn't help but mirror his feelings and become more engaged in science that year. This is because we all have something called mirror neurons that help us connect with others. When we see someone experience an emotion, it doesn't just register in our minds but also creates empathy and connection. Our own bodies begin to mirror or mimic what we are experiencing. This is why we can literally feel the pain of others and how we can benefit from being around super happy people as well.

When you enter the classroom excited, centered, and ready to share a learning experience with your students, they are picking this up in their bodies because of their mirror neurons. When you have taken the time to take care of yourself, you have a much better chance of being an energized and joyful teacher. If you are burnt out and beaten down, you are likely to expose your students to those same feelings, and everyone in the room ends up depleted and a little less excited about learning.

Your own well-being has a direct impact on your students. This is not just because of what you are modeling for them; you can also help them learn the same practices that help you take care of yourself. So many students, at younger and younger ages, are experiencing stress, anxiety, and depression. While no one expects you to become a therapist or miracle worker, you can offer students similar sorts of self-care practices that have helped you. Consider helping your students to do the following:

- Create some free time for themselves by learning to say no and unplugging for at least an hour a day.

- Talk to their parents about setting boundaries about social media, extracurricular activities, and other experiences that fill up every moment of their days.

- Create a more pleasant and enjoyable morning routine by going to bed earlier and getting up in time to do at least one thing that brings them joy before leaving for school.

- Pay attention to how they frame their experiences and how they might focus more on contribution rather than success or failure.

- Laugh more often and tell them not to take themselves so seriously.

One year when my husband, John, was teaching second grade, one of his students asked him, "What day is today?" John replied, "It is Thursday." The student cheered and said, "Yes! My favorite day. I don't have anything to do tonight. I can play and just be." If second graders are craving a little more free time, then I know our older students are starved for it. See how you can support your students and their families to find the kind of balance that helps them take the best care of themselves. This will ultimately lead to more happy families and more engaged students.

How might you focus more on your students' self-care? Which well-being practices are you going to put more attention into?

TEACH
BRAVELY

Video 7

Source: One 21 Production

It takes courage to grow up and become who you really are.

—e. e. cummings

During my first year as a professor of education, I taught a class that focused on content area literacy for preservice teachers who were also student teaching. About halfway through the semester, I was reading student work and writing feedback when I stumbled upon a folded-up note that fell out of a notebook. This student, Stephanie, had written a series of negative comments and insults about me back and forth with one of her friends. When I opened the note, I felt my face turning bright red, and a sense of shame, anger, and hurt rushed through my body. My first reaction was to contact this student and demand an apology. I wanted to put her in her place and tell her it was absolutely not okay to write disrespectful things about one's professor, especially me. I imagined how ashamed and shocked Stephanie would feel if she found out she accidentally handed in the note with her work. Instead, I took a few long breaths and calmed myself down.

I thought about what I learned from reading Brené Brown's (2012) book *Daring Greatly*, and I looked up at her leadership manifesto that was hanging above my desk. Her manifesto reminded me that the goal of a leader is to be courageous, to keep connection, and to humanize our work no matter what. I thought about how awful Stephanie would feel sitting across from me as I shamed her and how awful I would feel making her feel so badly. I just couldn't imagine a way this scenario would work out. The end result would likely be disconnection, mistrust, and an antagonistic relationship where we both did our best to get through the semester. I thought about the times I felt shamed by my teachers and how I couldn't learn from them no matter how smart they were and how much content they knew. So I decided to make a different choice.

I e-mailed Stephanie and asked her to come meet with me the next day. Then I spent the next twenty-four hours getting myself together and working on how I could have a vulnerable, honest conversation with her that left us both feeling more connected and committed to learning. I decided to let this conversation pique my curiosity about Stephanie and what was really going on for her. As Stephanie came into my office, I sat down next to her rather than across from her, showing her we are on the same team. I began by asking her how she was doing and how my class was going for her.

Stephanie replied, "It is fine," and then added, "What did you want to talk about?"

I took a breath and said, "Well, I wanted to make sure you are getting what you need from my class. I am here to teach you and support you, and I was thinking there may be some things that I could be doing that work better for you. How might I adjust the class for you?"

She looked surprised and said, "Nothing. Everything is good."

I could tell Stephanie was awkwardly trying to figure out what I was asking her and why. So I decided to meet her with even more empathy and directness, and I placed the note I had found in front of her on the table. I explained, "I found this note, and when I read it I realized you were not happy in my class. I really want to learn more about what would make my class work for you."

Stephanie's face grew purple and red. She began to cry. She said, "Oh my god. I can't believe you saw that note. I am so sorry."

Rather than berate her or make her feel badly, I leaned closer in and said, "While I was not happy to find this note, it helped me realize that we have not had a chance to talk about how things are going for you. If you feel the way you wrote in this note, then there must be some shifts I can make in our class. I really want to make it work for you."

We went on to have an honest conversation about how we were both feeling. She confided in me that she was not used to a class like mine—one where students have choice and agency and things are not always black and white. Then she said she was feeling so much pressure to get through her classes and juggle student teaching and that the day she passed the note she had a terrible day and was taking it out on me. She was passing the note with another student to vent and also to make her laugh. She said what she really needed was help with learning how to teach writing because she wanted to do well and support her future students. I explained that my feelings were hurt by the note but that talking about it together made me feel better and that my ultimate goal was for us to work together as a team to help her learn all she needed. We ended up hugging and agreeing she would come by during my office hours for help with writing instruction.

This was one of the hardest professional conversations I had with a student. It took so much courage and reflection for me to sit *with* her and to maintain my values and beliefs in the midst of a rather uncomfortable situation. There were so many other ways I could have used my position of power as the professor to humiliate or punish this student, and all of those would have broken our relationship and ultimately conflicted with my own core beliefs about teaching. The thing is, it is not always easy or comfortable to live my teaching beliefs and put them into action. There have been days I couldn't pull it off and days that it felt like a breeze. Some days I received some feedback on how it was going, but there were also many days when I was just not sure. In the case of this student, I did get some closure.

At the end of the semester, I received a thank-you card and gift from Stephanie on the day of her graduation. She thanked me for pushing her,

> I learned that teaching like myself means not just how I respond in the easy moments but also in the challenging ones.

for teaching her how to be the kind of teacher who cared about her students, and for modeling what it is like to give someone a second chance. It made me cry because I learned so much from her and that experience, and that I was so grateful our learning was mutual. I learned that teaching like myself meant being my whole self. It meant being vulnerable, real, and kind, especially in times of stress. I learned that teaching like myself means not just how I respond in the easy moments but also the challenging ones. I also was so thankful that I had Brown's leadership manifesto with me to remind me of how I wanted to choose to show up as a leader in that moment. I realized that there is much to lose if I don't choose to teach like myself.

WHAT DO WE LOSE IF WE DON'T TEACH LIKE OURSELVES?

I have reflected on my own experiences with teaching like someone else and doing what I thought I was supposed to do, rather than what I believed was right to do. I also spoke to many teachers about their experiences with being inauthentic, and I found three key repercussions of not teaching like yourself: We feel like imposters, our students can sense we are not being authentic, and our instructional decisions don't match our students.

Feeling Like an Imposter

While it is totally normal to feel like an imposter when we start something new, take a risk, and step into a new position, it can also totally debilitate our ability to bring out our best selves. Imposter syndrome is defined as "a belief that you're an inadequate and incompetent failure, despite evidence that indicates you're skilled and quite successful" (Wilding, n.d.). When we teach like someone else, like we think we are supposed to teach, rather than stay true to our own beliefs and practices, we often experience imposter syndrome. This leads to self-doubt, insecurity, and the feeling of being found out (Weir, 2013). When we are suffering from imposter syndrome, we tend to keep asking ourselves, "Am I doing it right?" This overthinking about whether it is right or not leads us to think in dualistic ways—black or white, right or wrong, and good or bad. This dualistic thinking leaves no room for ambiguity, ownership, and the gray area that real teaching and learning require. Our biggest fear when we are feeling like imposters is that we will be found out, called out, and never be able to show our faces again. In my experience, this imposter feeling is utterly unbearable, and I prefer to avoid it as much as possible.

Imposter syndrome can sneak up in small ways, like the time some Harvard graduate students were doing research in my classroom and observing my lessons. The fear that these Harvard folks would be judging me as not good enough took me out of my teaching flow. The whole time I was teaching I kept getting in my own head and thinking, "This is not good enough. What if they write about how terrible I am in their research study?" It didn't matter that they were studying the math program, not me; I couldn't stop feeling like I was going to be found out and humiliated.

Another time I outed myself publicly when I was feeling like an imposter. I was leading a session at the Learning and the Brain Conference, and I looked out and saw neuroscientists and professors in the audience. Even though I was an invited speaker, I felt like an imposter, which led to fear beginning to take over my body and brain. Instead of ignoring it and letting it take control, I started my talk by saying, "If I stumble over my words it is because I am feeling a bit out of my league...." People laughed, and by naming the imposter I was able to see it and move on. It lost a lot of its power as I brought awareness to it and kept on going because I began to settle into speaking like myself and not trying to be the scientist in the room. If you ever feel like an imposter, you are not alone.

Student Discomfort

When we are not teaching like ourselves, our students can sense it and are often quite uncomfortable. No students, no matter their age, feel safe or trust a teacher who is not being true to themselves. My own doctoral research included interviews with tenth graders about their experiences in English classes. Many students explained how awkward and unsettling it was when a teacher started to act in ways that felt inauthentic because they came across as "frontas." The students explained that a fronta is someone who acts one way on the outside and is really different on the inside. They claimed it was one of the worst traits a person could have. They came down quite harshly on anyone who would be a fronta because what they valued was being genuine. They couldn't trust a fronta (Goldberg, 2010).

Other ways that student discomfort comes with our own lack of authenticity show up more subtly. Sometimes students ask if we are okay. They look at us oddly and with a puzzled expression. Some students ask more direct questions like, "What are we supposed to do?" or "Is this something you have to make us do?" They sense our own discomfort with trying to be a teacher we are not and often respond with their own confusion.

One clear example of this was when I was in a classroom supporting a young teacher who was twenty-two years old. She was given a resource to use when teaching writing, and she felt the need to read from the book.

She placed the book on her lap and read the script exactly how it was written. One of the parts she read was a writing example about having to say goodbye to her son as he left home for the first time. Because she was reading from the book as if it was her own writing, a bunch of her students shouted out, "What? You have a son? How old is he? How old are you?" The students were so confused because clearly this twenty-two-year-old woman did not have a college-aged son. The teacher turned bright red and couldn't recover. She tried to explain that she misspoke, but it was too late. The students were so distracted by this inauthentic story that they missed the whole point of the lesson.

Missing the Mark

Sometimes when we are not teaching like ourselves it is not as obvious to our students, but we can see just how much we missed the mark with our instructional decisions. It could be that we found a lesson that looked good online or read about once in a professional book, but we didn't consider how to make it our own or how it would connect to our particular students. The number of times I have talked with teachers about a lesson that just didn't land right with students is too many to count. When I follow up by asking the teachers why they think the lesson didn't go so well, they almost always tell me it was because it did not match their students. When I dig a bit deeper with them, they often explain the lesson used a text the students didn't care about or connect with, or the lesson was too basic and the students were bored, or the lesson was too difficult and the students needed some background lessons first, or it felt out of the context of the larger classroom culture and therefore fell flat. Whatever the reason, when we are trying to teach someone else's lessons that were created for someone else's students, it rarely works and instead leaves us having to do even more teaching to get back on course.

What Do We Lose If We Don't Teach Like Ourselves?

★ We feel like imposters.

★ Our students can sense we are not being authentic.

★ Our instructional decisions don't match our students.

BE COURAGEOUS

My colleagues and friends from around the teaching world are all calling for a shift. Like me, they see the firsthand results of our recent educational climate focusing on testing, accountability, and standards, and missing the whole point of education—our actual students being happy and healthy. When we succumb to the pressure of outsiders and policy-makers who don't know our students, we are enrolling in their view of what counts. I have never met a single person who entered the teaching profession because they simply love data and tests; no, they love learning and they love children. As each teacher speaks up and chooses what is right for their particular students, we choose to teach bravely.

What we gain from teaching like ourselves is a healthy and happy class-room where every single person—we and our students—feels safe. People can't learn when they don't feel safe, and it is hard to feel safe when you don't feel welcome to show up as yourself. Imagine what it could be like if you entered the school each day feeling totally accepted and welcomed just as you are. I recently worked for an organization where the leader, Kelli, said this to us all on the first day: "We hired you to be you. We need you and your unique perspective on our team. We ask that you show up curious, vulnerable, genuine, and generous." I instantly relaxed into myself when I heard these words and I thought to myself, "My hope is that every teacher gets this message as they embark on each school year."

But what about all of us who don't have leaders who send us this mes-sage? If we wait for our administrators or boards of education to give us permission to be ourselves, some of us will be waiting a long time. I really don't believe this is because they don't believe we should be ourselves; instead, I think many leaders don't have this on their radar. They may be distracted by mandates, budgets, or parent phone calls, or they may have never had a leader who shared this same message with them. We can do this for ourselves and for our colleagues, though. I have seen firsthand, time and time again, how one person standing bravely as their true self can send ripples to all of their colleagues.

You can choose to be the teacher on the team who shows up as himself or herself. And if you make this choice, you are choosing to teach bravely. Embrace this role as the courageous, authentic teacher. Whether they state it or not, you will certainly inspire others around you. Recall from Chapter 6 that we all have mirror neurons that respond and reflect what others are experiencing around them. What do you want others to mir-ror from you? What do you want to model? How do you want to show up each day? I say, choose to be you.

Choose to Be Memorable

Still not sold? This sort of authenticity can be so scary. Think about the best teachers you had as a student, the ones who really left an imprint on you. What qualities did they possess? Were they just super smart or super organized? Did they stick to the mandated curriculum? Did they keep

> I have never met a single person who entered the teaching profession because they simply love data and tests; no, they love learning and they love children.

> Choose to be you.

a good grade book? I am sure none of those qualities were on your list. Instead, you likely listed some of these traits: thoughtful, caring, empathetic, creative, joyful, surprising, engaged, and genuine. If you want to be the teacher that your students remember with awe, then consider where you put most of your attention. What do you spend your time developing in your teaching? I doubt they will remember your test score passage rate. They will remember the time you listened as they struggled or when you shared your own vulnerable learning challenge with them and what you learned from it.

One of my favorite teachers was my third-grade teacher, Mr. Zax. He surprised me every day. I never knew what we would be doing in his class because it was not simply worksheets, quizzes, and assignments. In fact, I don't recall a single worksheet or ditto sheet from that year. I remember how he taught us physics by showing how to break a piece of wood in half with a karate chop. He loved karate. I remember how he let us write poems about whatever we wanted and how he would stop the class and have us read a powerful line from our poems to the rest of the class and let the words settle around us. I also remember quirky things like the way he wore the same suit every day to work. Once when a student asked him about it he winked at us. The next day he brought in three suits that were all identical and showed us that he wore the same suit because it fit him and was easy, but he had more than one. I wonder if Steve Jobs knew about Mr. Zax's strategy when he decided to make his clothing a uniform each day as well.

What I can say about Mr. Zax is that he was truly himself in the classroom. He was memorable. I never had a teacher quite like him again. This was not because he did gimmicky things but because he brought himself into the classroom and then gave us students a ton of space to do the same. That year I published one of my poems by writing it on a piece of wood, then staining it and giving it my mom for her Mother's Day gift. I am not sure why I wanted to do this, but it was totally acceptable to Mr. Zax that my poem be written on wood. He even suggested I add a piece of twine so my mom could hang it up. It may still be in my mom's kitchen all these years later.

Choose to Be Seen

In order to be yourself as a teacher, you are also choosing to be seen and to be exposed for who you really are. This means not everyone is going to like it. Being yourself doesn't mean that every student will list you as their favorite. Some of my best friends did not like being in Mr. Zax's class, but they all remember him and what he taught them. Being seen does not guarantee your colleagues will applaud your every idea. In fact, if being yourself challenges some of the norms of your grade level or team culture, they may react in less than ideal ways at first. But, as Brown (2017) writes in *Braving the Wilderness*, what we gain from being seen is much greater than what we stand to lose. She retells part of an interview with a pediatrician about how he handles the challenges of being seen as himself in his practice:

> Sometimes parents will get angry because I won't prescribe antibiotics for their child. The first thing they say is, "Every other pediatrician does it. I'll just go to someone else." It's not easy to hear this, but I always fall back on the thought, *It's okay if I'm alone on this. That's not what I believe is best for this child. Period.* (Brown, 2017, p. 27)

Brown goes on to recount what she learned from Maya Angelou about standing bravely as yourself. Angelou explained it this way:

> I belong to myself. I'm very proud of that. I am very concerned about how I look at Maya. I like Maya very much. I like the humor and courage very much. And when I find myself acting in a way that isn't… that doesn't please me—then I have to deal with that. (as quoted in Brown, 2017, p. 28)

What I take away from the interviews and stories Brown shares is how brave you really need to be in order to choose yourself. It sounds crazy on the surface, but it can be easier to be what others expect of you than to stand, for everyone to see, as the person you really are.

My guess, backed up by a lot of personal experience, is that most of us experienced some sort of shame as a child or teen when we were seen by our peers. This creates a sort of fear factor about choosing to do it again later in life. In his new book *Embarrassment*, Thomas Newkirk (2017) explains just how profound our early wounding is from being embarrassed and how it interferes with our ability to learn later on in life. He cites research conducted by David Pillemer, who found that we recall humiliating experiences with greater vividness than any other kind of memory, even positive ones (Newkirk, 2017, p. 12). This means that any previous experiences we had with being seen that led to being embarrassed are likely to have a large impact on our ability to choose to be seen authentically again. But Newkirk points out that none of us humans are immune to this fear. He writes, "None of us escapes the fear of performing poorly, ineptly, in public. All of us have done it at some point. We all deal—successfully or not—with fear of being seen as incompetent, even if the only person who sees this is ourselves" (p. 30). What I don't particularly like about Brown and Newkirk's research

> At the end of the day, we choose to be seen because it is often much more painful to hide and pretend to be someone we are not.

is the fact that just because we choose to be seen as our true selves, it does not guarantee it will work out, be successful, or lead to the result we desire. Nothing can guarantee success. At the end of the day, we choose to be seen because it is often much more painful to hide and pretend to be someone we are not.

Choose to Accept

A third brave choice we can make is to accept ourselves as we are. Again, this sounds easier than it may be in reality. If we hold ourselves to perfectionist standards and feel the need to please everyone in our lives, then accepting anything less feels like a failure. But no one is perfect, and no one is loved by everyone. If our self-acceptance is based on a bunch of if-thens, we can spend our entire lives and teaching careers chasing a dream that doesn't exist. Brown (2017) explains, "True belonging only happens when we present our authentic, imperfect selves to the world, our sense of belonging can never be greater than our level of self-acceptance" (p. 32). So if we want others to accept us—our students, colleagues, administrators, and community members—then we must begin with choosing self-acceptance.

Self-acceptance means being able to admit we are human, we make mistakes, we get it wrong, and we have beliefs that don't always align with everyone around us. We will sometimes make a decision that our teaching partners disagree with. We will teach a lesson in front of an administrator that doesn't go well. We will mess up a parent meeting and have to apologize and start over. We will call a student by the wrong name. We will be in a bad mood and take it out on others. When we accept that we will have good days and not so good days, but what matters most is being true to ourselves, we can make different and more impactful choices in the future. It is when we violate our own self-compass for what is right that we punish ourselves the most. We are all our worst critics. We come down the hardest on ourselves.

Be Courageous

★ Choose to be memorable.

★ Choose to be seen.

★ Choose to accept.

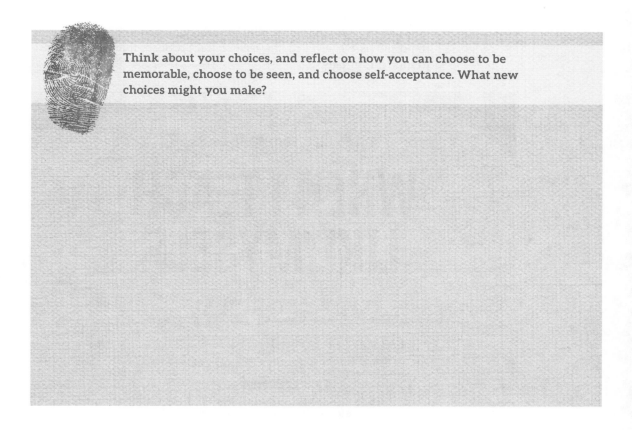

Think about your choices, and reflect on how you can choose to be memorable, choose to be seen, and choose self-acceptance. What new choices might you make?

TEACH LIKE YOURSELF MANIFESTO

I am ending this book with the Teach Like Yourself Manifesto because I want to help all teachers have a strong reminder of exactly what that means. While it is important to actually show up as yourself, it can be a huge benefit to also be able to put what that means into words. A manifesto is a declaration and a reminder. It calls us to action. During this time when there is pressure to teach like someone else from the media, politicians, and ill-informed policies, it is time for us teachers to speak up and show up. The best way to show the naysayers and so-called experts who don't really have a clue about what makes teaching the important craft it is, is for us to choose to teach like ourselves. We can say no to mandates that don't put students first. We can speak up when a new program takes priority over student learning. We can bravely align our practices and beliefs so that we teach in powerful and impactful ways.

When I teach like myself, I am saying NO to teaching like someone else. I am saying NO to mandates that do not work for my students, to choices that are not aligned with my beliefs, and to showing up as anything less than my most authentic self. The following manifesto can call us to stand tall as ourselves in the face of the pressures that often push us to shortcuts or fads.

Teach Like Yourself Manifesto

WHEN I TEACH LIKE MYSELF...

I START WITH WHY.
I make sure all of my teaching choices begin with my core beliefs.

I ALIGN MY TEACHING TO MY BELIEFS.
I view my teaching as a powerful practice I can hone each day.

I SEEK CONNECTION.
I build strong and balanced relationships with myself,
my students and their families, and my colleagues.

I GROW MY PRACTICE.
I drive my professional growth and look for opportunities to learn each day.

I TAKE CARE OF MYSELF.
I realize self-care, space, and my happiness have a
huge impact on the kind of teacher I can be.

I AM BRAVE.
I choose to show up as myself and accept that
this is exactly what my students deserve.

#teachlikeyourself
Gravity Goldberg
ISBN: 978-1-5443-3735-7
For more information, go to **corwin.com**

CORWIN
A SAGE Publishing Company

Please share this manifesto with your friends and anyone in your community who you believe needs to see it and hear its message.

THANK YOU

I want to personally thank you for being a teacher who chooses to be brave and show up as yourself. I truly and deeply believe that you are exactly what our children need. As a soon-to-be mother as well as a lifelong educator, I am so grateful for the teachers who choose authenticity. I know it is not always easy, and I know you will mess it up sometimes. Please know I am here cheering for you and believing in you. I am trying to create a new normal where teaching like yourself is the expected way tobe. I would love to hear from you about you. Take a final few minutes as you finish this book to reflect on exactly what it means for you right now to teach like yourself, and then please share it with me and the other teachers in the world who need to see it. Tweet your reflection to me at @drgravityg with the hashtag #teachlikeyourself, or e-mail me at gravity@drgravitygoldberg.com. I can't wait to hear your story. Thank you.

What does it mean for YOU to teach like yourself?

APPENDIX
BOOK STUDY GUIDE

The following questions are meant to offer you suggestions for how to reflect on the learning from each chapter. I suggest you alternate between independent time to reflect on your own and time with your colleagues to reflect together. You may want to view the videos that go along with each chapter with your colleagues before you begin your discussions. Following each set of reflection questions is an extra challenge. The challenges are meant for you to take some immediate action. Have fun with them, and playfully lean into whatever comes. They are called challenges because they may push your edges a bit. That is likely where the most impactful learning will happen. Don't feel the need to do all of this or to do this in the order presented here. Make it your own. Choose the questions and challenges that speak loudest to you. Add in your own, and change the sequence to match your most pressing goals.

CHAPTER 1

- What would the people across my entire life say is my most unique strength?

- Apart from what others might say, what do I consider my most unique talent or strength?

- How does my authentic self show up in the classroom?

- **Challenge:** Ask your students to name and list your unique strengths as a teacher. Then ask your colleagues and mentors to do the same. Take ownership of the list.

CHAPTER 2

- What are my core beliefs about teaching?

- What are my core beliefs about learning?

- Is there a person I attribute my core beliefs to—a parent or a mentor, or a body of work or research?

- What or who nourishes my beliefs?
- **Challenge:** Make your own Golden Circle, and list your why, how, and what. Then share it with your colleagues, and ask for feedback on how much this seems true to them as your learning partners.

CHAPTER 3

- How do my current teaching practices align with my core beliefs?
- What is one topic I want to practice deliberately? How might I make my students aware of it so they can be part of the practice?
- When in my life did I feel personally powerful? What were the conditions? Was I alone or with others?
- How do colleagues enhance my moments of personal power? What do they do or say?
- How might I act to bring about more frequent powerful moments as a teacher?
- How might I create the conditions for students to have these same moments of feeling powerful?
- **Challenge:** Create a priming routine, and practice it for at least two weeks straight daily. Record how it went each day. Then examine its impact on your sense of personal power.

CHAPTER 4

- What is working well in terms of my relationships at school? With colleagues? With students?
- What do I consider a core strength when it comes to developing positive communication?
- What is a possible aspect of relationship-building I want to get better at?
- Who do I feel most in conflict with at school, and how can I apply the strategies in this chapter to bring about a more constructive relationship?
- **Challenge:** Initiate and create a celebration of some kind with your students and/or colleagues. Notice how the relationship feels before and after.

CHAPTER 5

- What helps me to succeed in meeting goals?

- Is there someone at school who I know would be a motivating person for my professional growth?

- Is there a student I've taught that, for whatever reason, I feel I was less than effective with? How can I use that experience to set a professional learning goal?

- If I could take a year-long sabbatical and study anything, anywhere, what might that be? How might I connect this dream to professional growth plans this year?

- **Challenge:** Host a book club. Form a group, find a text, and facilitate some professional learning experiences with your colleagues.

CHAPTER 6

- How did I initially respond to reading the chapter on caring for myself? What might that mean?

- What is that recording that loops through my brain, getting in the way of my self-care? If I could put it in a single sentence, what would it be—and how can I turn this "I can't" mindset into "I can"?

- What boundaries do I want to create for myself? How will I do this?

- Which aspects of self-care did I most connect with, and how might I make it a reality for myself?

- How can I help my students take better care of themselves?

- **Challenge:** Enlist some colleagues in forming a Rule Number 6 Club so you help each other not to take yourselves too seriously. Have fun creating some joyful experiences with one another such as watching comedy videos, practicing laughter yoga, or simply doing something fun together on a regular basis just because it brings you happiness.

CHAPTER 7

- What would my own Teach Like Yourself Manifesto say?

- What qualities do I think my students will remember most about me?

- How am I hiding a bit of my true teacher self? What would it look like to show up a bit more as myself?

- How can I choose to accept myself even more than I do right now?

- How do I describe myself as an educator?

- If I had to give a brand-new teacher a single sentence of advice, what would it be?

- **Challenge:** Make a one-minute video of yourself explaining what it means for you to teach like yourself. Tweet it with the hashtag #teachlikeyourself, post it on our group Facebook page (https://www.facebook.com/groups/teachlikeyourself), and then tag another teacher and enlist him or her to do the same.

JOIN THE *TEACH LIKE YOURSELF* MOVEMENT

Please join our *Teach Like Yourself* movement, proudly speaking up to show just how important it is to honor each and every teacher's authentic self. Here are some ways to share your beautifully unique teacher self.

- Join our Facebook community group: https://www.facebook.com/groups/teachlikeyourself.

- Tweet about your teacher self by using the hashtag #teachlikeyourself.

- Post the manifesto poster proudly in your classroom or office.

- Give a copy of the book to a teacher friend.

- Participate in a book club, and share your learning with your colleagues.

- Make a one-minute video telling us what it means for you to teach like yourself. Share that video on social media using the hashtag #teachlikeyourself.

- Show up each day, ready to bring your most authentic and real teacher self.

REFERENCES

Achor, S. (2010). *The happiness advantage*. New York, NY: Random House.

Atwell, N. (1989). *In the middle: A lifetime of learning about writing, reading, and adolescents* (3rd ed.). Portsmouth, NH: Heinemann.

Bandura, A. (1977). *Social learning theory*. Englewood Cliffs, NJ: Prentice Hall.

Bellock, S. (2015). *How the body knows the mind: The surprising power of the physical environment to influence how you think and feel*. New York, NY: Atria Books.

Bohm, D. (2004). *On dialogue*. New York, NY: Routledge.

Brown, B. (2012). *Daring greatly: How the courage to be vulnerable transforms the way we live, love, parent, and lead*. New York, NY: Avery.

Brown, B. (2015). *Own our history. Change the story* [Web log post]. Retrieved from https://brenebrown.com/blog/2015/06/18/own-our-history-change-the-story

Brown, B. (2017). *Braving the wilderness: The quest for true belonging and the courage to stand alone*. New York, NY: Random House.

Calkins, L. (1994). *The art of teaching writing*. Portsmouth, NH: Heinemann.

Cochran, T. (2013, April 8). Email is not free. *Harvard Business Review*.

Csikszentmihalyi, M. (1990). *Flow: The science of optimal experience*. New York, NY: HarperPerennial.

Cuddy, A. (2015). *Presence: Bringing your boldest self to your biggest challenges*. New York, NY: Little, Brown.

Dalai Lama, Tutu, D., & Abrams, D. (2016). *The book of joy*. New York, NY: Avery.

Deci, E., & Ryan, R. (2000). Self-determination theory and the facilitation of intrinsic motivation, social development, and well-being. *American Psychologist, 55*(1), 68–78.

Deresiewicz, W. (2014). *Excellent sheep: The miseducation of the American elite and the way to a meaningful life*. New York, NY: Free Press.

Donohoo, J. (2016). *Collective efficacy: How educators' beliefs impact student learning.* Thousand Oaks, CA: Corwin.

Dweck, C. (2007). *Mindset: The new psychology of success.* New York, NY: Ballantine Books.

Education International. (2017, August 3). Early stage teachers. Retrieved from https://www.ei-ie.org/en/detail_page/4644/early-stage-teachers

Eisenberger, N., Lieberman M., & Williams K. (2003). Does rejection hurt? An FMRI study of social exclusion. *Science, 302*(5643), 290–292.

Ferlazzo, L. (2012). *To sell is human: The surprising truth about moving others.* New York, NY: Riverhead Books.

Frankl, V. E. (1959). *Man's search for meaning.* Boston, MA: Beacon Press.

Gable, S. L., Reis, H. T., Impett, E. A., & Asher, E. R. (2004). What do you do when things go right? The intrapersonal and interpersonal benefits of sharing positive events. *Journal of Personality and Social Psychology, 87,* 228–245.

Gallagher, K. (2009). *Readicide: How schools are killing reading and what you can do about it.* York, ME: Stenhouse.

Godin, S. (2012, October 16). *Stop stealing dreams* [Video file]. Retrieved from https://www.youtube.com/watch?v=sXpbONjV1Jc

Godin, S. (2014). *Tribes: We need you to lead us.* London, England: Piatkus Books.

Godin, S. (2017a). *Everyone else is irrational* [Web log post]. Retrieved from http://sethgodin.typepad.com/seths_blog/2017/11/everyone-else-is-irrational.html

Godin, S. (2017b). *Two kinds of practice* [Web log post]. Retrieved from http://sethgodin.typepad.com

Goldberg, G. (2010). *High school students' experiences in a newly participatory English classroom* [Doctoral dissertation]. Teachers College, Columbia University, , New York, NY.

Goldberg, G. (2015). *Mindsets and moves: Strategies that help readers take charge.* Thousand Oaks, CA: Corwin.

Gonzalez, J. (2016, September 25). *How pineapple charts revolutionize professional development.* Retrieved from https://www.cultofpedagogy.com/pineapple-charts

Gottman, J. (2017). *The magic relationship ratio* [Web log post]. Retrieved from https://www.gottman.com/blog/the-magic-relationship-ratio-according-science

Gray, P. (2010, January 26). The decline of play and rise in children's mental disorders. *Psychology Today*. Retrieved from https://www .psychologytoday.com/blog/freedom-learn/201001/the-decline-play-and-rise-in-childrens-mental-disorders

Gray, P. (2013). *Free to learn: Why unleashing the instinct to play will make our children happier, more self-reliant, and better students for life*. New York, NY: Basic Books.

Greenville-Cleave, B. (2012). *Positive psychology: A practical guide*. Toronto, ON: Penguin Books.

Hargreaves, A., & Fullan, M. (2012). *Professional capital: Transforming teaching in every school*. New York, NY: Teachers College Press.

Hattie, J. (2016). 195 influences and effect sizes related to student achievement. Retrieved from https://visible-learning.org/hattie-ranking-influences-effect-sizes-learning-achievement

Huston, T. (2013). Why it is called a yoga practice. Retrieved from https://www.elephantjournal.com/2013/01/why-its-called-a-yoga-practice-trish-huston

Joyce, B., & Showers, B. (2002). Student achievement through professional development. In B. Joyce & B. Showers (Eds.), *Designing training and peer coaching: Our need for learning*. Alexandria, VA: ASCD.

Knight, J. (2007). *Instructional coaching: A partnership approach to improving instruction*. Thousand Oaks, CA: Corwin.

Langer, E. (2016). *The power of mindful learning*. Boston, MA: Da Capo Lifelong Books.

Leana, C. R. (2011, Fall). The missing link in school reform. *Stanford Social Innovation Review*.

Lobel, A. (2004). *Days with Frog and Toad*. New York, NY: HarperCollins.

National School Public Relations Association. (2011, August 26). National survey pinpoints communication preferences in school communication. Retrieved from https://www.nspra.org/files/docs/Release%20on%20CAP%20Survey.pdf

Newkirk, T. (2017). *Embarrassment: And the emotional underlife of learning*. Portsmouth, NH: Heinemann.

Newport, C. (2016). *Deep work: Rules for focused success in a distracted world*. New York, NY: Grand Central Publishing.

Noel, A., Stark, P., Redford, J., & Zukerberg, A. (2013). *Parent and family involvement in education, from the National Household Education Surveys Program of 2012*. Washington, DC: U.S. Department of Education.

Palmer, P. (1998). *The courage to teach: Exploring the inner landscape of the teacher's life*. San Francisco, CA: Jossey-Bass.

Pink, D. H. (2012). *To sell is human: The surprising truth about moving others*. New York, NY: Riverhead Books.

Pope, D. C. (2003). *Doing school: How we are creating a generation of stressed-out, materialistic, and miseducated students*. New Haven, CT: Yale University Press.

Prinstein, M. (2015). The psychology of popularity: An interview with Dr. Mitch Prinstein. Retrieved from https://positivepsychologyprogram .com/the-psychology-of-popularity-an-interview-with-dr-mitch-prin- stein

Protheroe, N. (2008). Teacher efficacy: What is it and does it matter? *Principal, 87*(5), 42–45.

Public Agenda. (2012). Parents want to be involved in children's edu- cation yet don't understand key factors affecting public educa- tion quality. Retrieved from https://www.publicagenda.org/pages/ engaging-parents

Quaglia Student Voice Survey. (2016). Retrieved from https://surveys .quagliainstitute.org

Reeve, J. (2002). Self-determination theory applied to educational set- tings. In E. L. Deci & R. M. Ryan (Eds.), *Handbook of self-determination research* (pp. 183–203). Rochester, NY: University of Rochester Press.

Reynolds, J. (2018). *Daily Show* interview. Retrieved from http://www .cc.com/video-clips/avk8pe/the-daily-show-with-trevor-noah-jason- reynolds–serving-young-readers-with–long-way-down

Rubin, G. (2015). *The happiness project: Or, why I spent a year trying to sing in the morning, clean my closets, fight right, read Aristotle, and generally have more fun*. New York, NY: Harper Paperbacks.

Seligman, M. (2006). *Learned optimism: How to change your mind and your life*. New York, NY: Vintage.

Sinek, S. (2009). *Start with why: How great leaders inspire everyone to take action*. New York, NY: Portfolio.

Stanier, M. B. (2016). *The coaching habit: Say less, ask more, and change the way you lead forever*. Toronto, Canada: Box of Crayons Press.

Tracy, B. (2010). *How the best leaders lead: Proven secrets to getting the most out of yourself and others*. New York, NY: Amacom.

Twenge, J., Gentile, B., DeWall, C. N., Ma, D., Lacefield, K., & Schurtz, D. R. (2010). Birth cohort increases in psychopathology among young Americans, 1938–2007: A cross-temporal meta-analysis of the MMPI. *Clinical Psychology Review, 30*(2), 145–154.

Vanderkam, L. (2012). *What the most successful people do before breakfast: And two other short guides to achieving more at work and at home.* New York, NY: Portfolio.

Weir, K. (2013, November). Feel like a fraud? *gradPSYCH Magazine, 11* (4). Retrieved from http://www.apa.org/gradpsych/2013/11/fraud.aspx

Wilding, M. J. (n.d.). 5 different types of imposter syndrome (and 5 ways to battle each one). *The Muse.* Retrieved from https://www.themuse.com/advice/5-different-types-of-imposter-syndrome-and-5-ways-to-battle-each-one

Zander, B., & Zander, R. (2002). *The art of possibility: Transforming professional and personal life.* New York, NY: Penguin Books.

INDEX

Helping educators make the *greatest impact*

Corwin books represent the latest thinking from some of the most respected experts in K–12 education. We are proud of the breadth and depth of the books we have published and the authors we have partnered with in our mission to better serve educators and students.

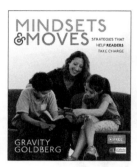

GRAVITY GOLDBERG

Let go of the default roles of assigner, monitor, and manager and shift to a growth mindset. The 4 Ms framework lightens your load by allowing students to monitor and direct their own reading lives.

GRAVITY GOLDBERG RENEE HOUSER

Learn how focusing on relationships, clarity, and challenge can put you in control of managing your classroom's success, one motivated student at a time.

SERENA PARISER

This handy guide offers 50 proven best practices for managing today's classroom, complete with just-in-time tools and relatable teacher-to-teacher anecdotes and advice.

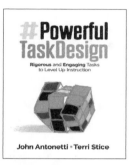

JOHN ANTONETTI TERRI STICE

This book will teach you to use the Powerful Task Rubric for Designing Student Work to analyze, design, and refine engaging tasks of learning.

LISA WESTMAN

Full of step-by-step guidance, this book shows you how to build collaborative student-teacher relationships and incorporate student voice and choice in the process of planning for student-driven differentiation.

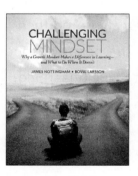

JAMES NOTTINGHAM BOSSE LARSSON

Create the right conditions for a growth mindset to flourish in your school and your students.

JILL NOTTINGHAM JAMES NOTTINGHAM

Jumpstart meaningful learning for students with new Learning Challenge lessons.

To order your copies, visit corwin.com

A SAGE Publishing Company

Helping educators make the greatest impact

CORWIN HAS ONE MISSION: to enhance education through intentional professional learning.

We build long-term relationships with our authors, educators, clients, and associations who partner with us to develop and continuously improve the best evidence-based practices that establish and support lifelong learning.